Below the Rim

FOOTSTEPS THROUGH THE GRAND CANYON

Dottie Fox

Dottie Fox

WHO PRESS · BASALT, COLORADO

PUBLISHED BY

WHO Press
0311 West Sopris Creek Road
Basalt, Colorado 81621

Library of Congress Control Number: 00-133757
ISBN 1-882426-15-0
Printed in the United States of America

Cover Illustration by Dottie Fox
Cover Design by Curt Carpenter
Editing by Warren H. Ohlrich

Like winds and sunsets, wild things were taken for granted until progress began to do away with them. Now we face the question whether a still higher "standard of living" is worth its cost in things natural, wild and free. For us of the minority, the opportunity to see geese is more important than television, and the chance to find a pasque-flower is a right as inalienable as free speech.

— Aldo Leopold, *A Sand County Almanac*

Leave it as it is . . . the ages have been at work on it and man can only mar it.

— Theodore Roosevelt

TO RANDY AND MURRAY,
TWO VERY SPECIAL
PERSONS.

Table of Contents

Preface

Through my years of backpacking in the Grand Canyon, various friends have been along, but as time progressed there emerged a faithful threesome: Murray, Randy and I. Our itineraries became increasingly selective and more difficult, with trips lasting ten or more days at a time. Friends became less interested.

There is always the temptation to lure friends and relatives into a place you happen to think is wonderful and then, after you have convinced them to join you on a trip, you begin to wonder how wise a decision was made. It's too easy to tell about the adventure, beauty and majesty of the Canyon, but somehow to minimize the long waterless miles, the impossible heavy pack, the heat and often the cold. I love the emptiness and the isolation, but I've found that those attributes aren't high on the list of favorite things for most people.

So it seems that, more often than not, our faithful threesome will venture out together once more, especially when exploring areas new to us. Randy, a poet and wilderness lover, is my son. Murray first climbed mountains in New Hampshire at the age of four. He was a hiker, backpacker and long-time friend and neighbor in Old Snowmass.

As for me, Colorado has always been my home, and once my four children were old enough to either come along or be left at home, I was off exploring the Colorado Rockies. Then came the deserts, plateaus and canyons of Utah and Arizona, and at last the Grand Canyon.

There have been hiking trips to New Zealand, Alaska and Scotland, which were wonderful and exciting, but nothing for me has equaled my many treks below the rim in the Grand Canyon of the Colorado River.

Introduction

I am about to have my very first look at one of earth's most famous places. With mounting excitement, I join dozens of other tourists walking out to a viewpoint on the South Rim.

I have seen photographs, paintings and movies portraying the Grand Canyon, so I have a good idea of what to expect. But now I will see it in person. Suddenly, I'm on the rim and there it is! I look down, I look up and across. I keep looking as the babble of voices comes and goes around me. I keep looking, as the late sun turns the tops of the highest pinnacles a bright vermillion, leaving long shadows stretching to the east. Somewhere in the cool, blue purple of the cavernous canyon below is the Colorado River, the perpetual sculptor of this long gash in Mother Earth.

I try to remember all I've heard and read. The length is over 200 miles; it's 9–12 miles from rim to rim, depending upon where you are; 5,000–6,000 feet from top to bottom. It's a 215-mile drive from the North Rim to the South Rim and the whole represents a geological timetable which stretches back 250 million to 2 billion years, deep in the Inner Gorge.

I gaze out over the Canyon looking for a familiar landmark. The facts are forgotten as I look down into the depths again. Comprehension escapes me; I drop down from the edge, away from the tourist confusion, and sit on a rock outcropping. Instantly, it's unbelievably quiet. The Canyon lies around and below, mystical and eternal. I feel strangely detached. As the sun sinks lower, the blazing reds become subdued and a purple haze rises to absorb the pink towers and buttes. An unreal hush covers all. A shiny black raven skims overhead with a soft swish of its wings. Time stands still. Silence is everywhere.

I get up slowly and force myself to leave. I look back once more and realize I have seen the Grand Canyon. All the pictures, all the information, every preconceived idea I'd ever had — all disappear and become meaningless. Maybe when I come back and look again, I can make sense out of the facts and figures, but now, even though I've only had a small glimpse, the magic has touched me and I have an indescribable urge to enter this world of grandeur and mystery.

And so begins a long relationship with the Canyon. As a hiker and backpacker, it was impossible not to want to explore the trails into this wonder of the world. Many years have passed since that memorable day. And now over 250 days have been spent hiking and backpacking in the Canyon, including a twelve-day, oar-powered river raft trip.

Each trip has been different and special and, having kept a journal on each, I decided that one day I wanted to put it all into a book. This is certainly not a history book nor a guidebook, although some bits of information may be of use to backpackers, but a personal, sometimes a bit emotional, record where I and others can relive those experiences in the Canyon and provide an encouraging word for those who are about to enter this world of wonderment for the first time.

Many trails I have done more than once, but I have chosen a few of the outstanding trips which to me best represent the adventure, the beauty, the agony and the ecstasy of backpacking in the Grand Canyon. Let this be a tribute to an incredible place!

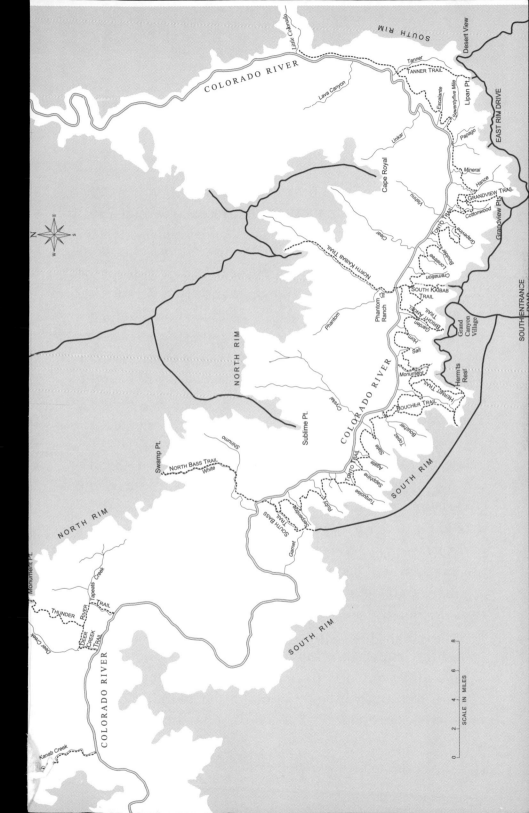

CHAPTER 1

First Time Below the Rim

South Kaibab and Bright Angel Trails • September 1976

FIRST DAY

As an introduction to the Grand Canyon, two women friends and I choose a popular tourist trail, just east of Grand Canyon Village, for our first venture into the amazing world below. At the South Kaibab Trailhead we hikers from Colorado discuss how strange it seems to be starting with heavy packs and going down to our destination instead of up. But hopefully those packs will be lighter three days from now, when we climb up the Bright Angel Trail and out of the Canyon.

Eight miles to the river, downhill all the way. Doesn't sound too bad until we lift up the packs, each with a gallon of water weighing a miserable eight pounds. The next shock comes almost immediately as the trail suddenly seems to drop off into space. We negotiate the upper switchbacks gingerly, as we try to adjust to the weight of our packs and the not so stable trail below our feet.

Finally we get past the mechanics of hiking enough to realize where we are. The day is sparkling and warm, everything is a rosy pink as the light reflects off the Hermit Shale. At last I'm entering the magical land of the Grand Canyon. What a different world from the spruce-filled forests, icy streams and snowcapped mountains of Colorado. The stark simplicity, the economy of vegetation, the dryness and the

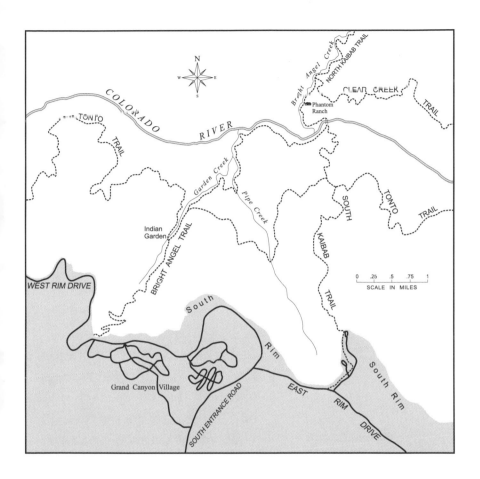

flamboyant desert colors surrounding me are new and exciting. Now and then a wildflower appears along the trail to add a spot of brilliant yellow, blue or white to its rose-colored environment.

Many careful, downhill steps later and we reach the Redwall. This great limestone formation is a vertical cliff often more than 500 feet high that presents a formidable obstacle in much of the Canyon. The various trails lead through breaks in the wall, some more difficult than others, but usually steep and rocky. The brilliant red color is only a superficial stain of iron oxide which, through the ages, has trickled down over the grey rock from the truly red formations above — the Hermit Shale and Supai Sandstone.

The temperature begins to climb and our canteens get lighter as we ration the precious tepid water. The trail continues down, down unrelentingly and toes complain as they push against the boots with every step. The pack remains an uncomfortable load on my hot back and my knees seem permanently bent as our threesome covers the dusty, hot miles to the river. Again my body sensations are beginning to overshadow what I'm here to see and experience. As I look out over this land of rock sculptures shimmering in the afternoon heat, it all becomes unreal.

Barrel Cactus

The narrow suspension footbridge over the Colorado River is finally just below us, a sure sign that we're reaching the end of the trail. As the high walls of the Canyon reach up around us, it becomes unbearably hot. What seemed like the end of the day a while ago still stretches on past Phantom Ranch and finally across a creek to the campground. The monster on my back slides to the ground, off come the dusty boots and socks as I head for the bubbly, clear waters of Bright Angel Creek. What an appropriate name Major Powell gave to this cheerful stream!

So here we are in the bottom of the Grand Canyon. Somehow I thought that once I reached this deep abyss it would be claustrophobic and somber, but quite the opposite. The gift of water in Bright Angel Creek, along with the mighty Colorado River has turned the desert into an oasis, with cottonwood trees and lush vegetation. Along the Colorado, just a short way behind the campground, graceful tamarisks line the shore. Wildflowers and flowering bushes mix with various species of cacti and tall grasses growing in the sandy soil.

At last the blistering sun drops behind the high walls which tower above. It's time to unroll the foam pad, rest our tired muscles, look at the azure sky and just be in the Grand Canyon. We have dropped from the cool forest of the South Rim 4,800 feet to a tropical environment at 2,500 feet.

No more just looking over the rim. I'm here, and as my toes and knees begin to revive, the old yen to explore begins to surface. My two companions join me in a walk along the Colorado River. A pleasant wind blows across the sandy beach as the tall grasses sway leaving their circular patterns in the sand and the pink flowered tamarisks bend low over the water's edge.

There are many hikers in the campground. Picnic tables are even provided, and beer, food and lodging are available at Phantom Ranch. The unfamiliar sounds of different foreign languages drift over from various campsites. As darkness descends, tiny spots of light dot the blackness as campers cook their meals over little stoves. Bedtime comes early for most as sleepy eyes wait for the stars to appear in the narrow banner of ebony sky overhead.

SECOND DAY

Morning brings pleasant and welcome shade, for the sun must work its way overhead before this narrow strip of land gets its rays. I lie in my bag and chuckle as my friend Gracie crawls out on hands and knees and slowly heads for a picnic table to pull herself up! Forty-eight hundred vertical feet downhill takes its toll on legs and knees. Another hiker walks stiff-legged to the creek for water. I stop laughing when I try to get out of my bag.

But sore knees or not, we're ready to find out what's in this amazing place. We walk past Phantom Ranch to where several river boats have just arrived with a hubbub of activity and decide to hike up the Clear Creek Trail, a well-constructed trail up to and along the Tonto Plateau. It is nine miles east to Clear Creek itself — long, dry and tedious — but today we'll go only a few miles. The views are spectacular, looking down 1,000 feet to the silver ribbon of the Colorado River twisting gracefully between the dark walls of the Canyon.

As the trail winds below a tremendous rock wall and Zoroaster Temple looms directly ahead, I begin to sense more isolation than I'd experienced yesterday. No other travelers pass us, the vastness ahead looks wild and untrammeled by humans. Lunch is on a lonely plateau high above the deep, dark Inner Gorge. That exquisite silence surrounds us as the Canyon magic begins to cast its spell.

As Connie, Gracie and I make our way down the trail back to the Phantom Ranch Campground, my mind is busy wondering what we might have found, had we continued to Clear Creek. Was it as wild and isolated as it appeared in the distance? What sort of vistas from the Tonto would we have seen? Was Clear Creek an intermittent stream or bubbling cascade of water leaving a green oasis beside its life-giving water? All these unanswered questions swirl about my head and I know that this will be the next trail I must take.

Another night at our busy campsite. As I look at all the campers preparing their evening meals and hear their chatter of voices, I try to imagine what it must be like at Clear Creek without this bustle of activity, with only the song of the birds, the rustle of the leaves and the evening cricket serenade. My appetite has been whetted by this first taste of the Inner Canyon and I know I will be back.

THIRD DAY

The route back to the South Rim winds eleven miles up the Bright Angel Trail, very different from the South Kaibab, with plenty of water and much more vegetation. Our plan is to break up the long, eleven-mile hike out and camp at Indian Gardens, a green haven with majestic cottonwood trees. Many years ago the Havasupai Indians used to grow crops here, where campers now set up their tents. A pleasant place to camp under the spreading trees, with not quite the busy pace of the Phantom Ranch Campground.

FOURTH DAY

Four and one-half miles to the rim from Indian Gardens gives our uphill muscles a chance to work. Every now and then we must stop and step out on the downhill side of the trail to let the mule trains go by. These sure-footed beasts of burden are a big attraction for those unwilling or unable to hike the Canyon. Faces of the riders portray every emotion—from fear and trembling, to stoic toleration of the situation, to complete enjoyment. An amusing afternoon's entertainment is to wait at the South Rim corral for the mule trips to arrive home and then watch as each rider dismounts. Once I watched some poor woman get helped off to the ground and simply stand there with slightly bowed legs, completely immobilized, until someone gently encouraged her to put one foot in front of the other and led her away. Ah, the Canyon experience!

The trail is wide and well constructed here, but originally it was a prehistoric Indian route. Prospectors improved it and charged tourists a toll for its use, until finally the Park Service took it over. Millions of years ago the Bright Angel Fault lifted the strata to the west, and it is this break through the cliff that makes the route possible. We now reach the first of two tunnels and more people are coming and going, since this upper part is a short, popular hike for those with limited time or energy.

A few more switchbacks, as we look down on the distant strip of green in Indian Gardens, and we are on the rim. We are feeling very pleased with ourselves as our packs slide to the ground. It was a long way down and back, but it was pleasant to have broken the trip into four days, rather than racing down and back, which is often the way of hikers going in for the first time.

As we take the final snapshots of each other I walk over to the edge and, looking down into those shadowy depths, I remember my first glimpse of the Canyon. Yes, it is still awe-inspiring, beautiful, mysterious, a bit intimidating; but now I've been in there at last and I feel a little more rapport with it, perhaps have even a bit more understanding of what I'm looking at and, again, I know without a shadow of a doubt that I will be coming back below the rim.

CHAPTER 2

Near Disaster—Happy Ending

Deer Creek and Thunder River • October 1979

After hearing Murray relate the glories of the Grand Canyon, a little spark of interest was ignited in his daughter and son-in-law, and it was finally decided that we would all do a North Rim trip in October. This was a new one for us too, but since Cynthia and Jack were young and in good shape from running marathons, Randy, Murray and I felt confident about it.

FIRST DAY

After a night spent at the North Rim Campground, packing backpacks, figuring our meals for six days, and filling all the plastic bottles for the dry trip of over ten miles down to Deer Creek, we leave the paved rim road and drive the twenty miles of dirt road to Monument Point. Here the cars will be left and the trail begins. There's excitement in the air—a new trail, new companions along, but with just one worry, the state of my health. A week before I had a severe allergic reaction and am still light-headed, dizzy and definitely not in tiptop condition. But being an eternal optimist and determined to go, with shaky knees I join the others down the steep trail. The temperature is very hot for early October and a final word from the Backcountry Office was, "Don't get caught in Surprise Valley at noon!"

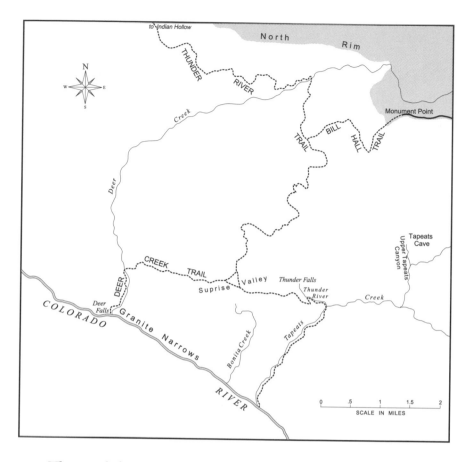

The trail drops 1,000 feet through the Kaibab and Coconino formations in one mile, then circles west and south along the Esplanade to the top of the Redwall, where it drops close to another 1,000 feet into Surprise Valley. It's still early, so the temperature is bearable until we reach the Redwall and are suddenly confronted with a raging furnace as the heat radiates off the red rock cliffs. Everyone is beginning to wilt, but especially me. I look for an excuse to stop and sit in the shade under an overhang, and I'm tempted to drain my canteen at every stop. We are all slow today and I'm not helping. Somehow I force my legs to move, but my head is throbbing as I seem to go slower and slower. Murray finally tells the others to go on, that we will meet them after Surprise Valley or at Deer Creek.

We rest often, as I realize that at any moment I may pass out, and then, horror of horrors, Murray tells me that we are in Surprise Valley at noon! The temperature is 115 degrees with not a bush or boulder in sight. Murray checks out the indefinite trail which divides here, one branch going to Thunder River, the other to Deer Creek. I slide to the ground, trying desperately to find a little shade from my pack. As the heat intensifies, the world is whirling around and I realize weakly that I may not make it out of here. That very thought sends a little adrenaline through me and I get to my feet. Murray helps me on with my pack and somehow my legs shakily carry me along. Everything is very vague — in the distance I seem to be hearing Murray say that we must find shade and that we can't stop until we do.

Next thing I remember is huddling under a large boulder, drinking the little remaining water in my canteen. Worried Murray, who hadn't realized how far "out of it" I really was, has decided we will wait here until the sun sets before going on to Deer Creek, all of which is fine with me. I just want to lie down and never go anywhere again.

Time passes as in a dream. I hear Murray talking, but I don't understand the words. Somehow I'm walking again and the sun has gone and it seems to be getting darker. Then I realize that Randy is here, has taken my pack, and the three of us are going somewhere. Now my pack is on again and someone far away mentions Deer Creek as I carefully pick my way down a very steep, boulder-strewn trail. The temperature has cooled off and my head is beginning to clear a bit. As I consciously focus my eyes, I realize that we have reached our campsite at Deer Creek and there sit two very forlorn friends, Cynthia and Jack, wondering how all this is going to end. I suppose I had dinner, but all I want to do is curl up in my bag and sleep.

SECOND DAY

I open my eyes to the morning, feeling relaxed and rested. I remember yesterday as though it were a bad dream. I'm up! I can feel all eyes on me, wondering if I'm suddenly going to topple over. I feel great, I'm hungry and I'm ready to go hiking! Some wonderful miracle has happened and, as we try to analyze it, our conclusion is that all the toxins from the allergic reaction in my system were sweated out by the intense heat of yesterday. Who knows whether this is a scientific explanation that would satisfy the medical profession, but it's past history now and we have a day in camp and an easy hike to the river and Deer Falls.

Spirits are definitely on the upswing now. Without the heavy packs, we hike the mile or so down to the Colorado River. We go up a charming little canyon and there is Deer Falls, dropping 200 feet in a sparkling plume of water straight down to a deep azure pool. We stand in awe as the cool spray, filled with the colors of the rainbow, envelops us. Then suddenly off come the clothes as bodies frolic under the powerful waterfall which roars its watery welcome. A fairyland for sure, with delicate, green maidenhair fern growing thickly on the nearby rocks. Another joy of the desert is to find this enchanted oasis after the heat and desolation of Surprise Valley.

Lunch is eaten on the white sand under the tamarisks by the river. No hurry today. Plenty of time to let the sand shape to one's body, to simply lie there, watching the water flow by on its way to the Gulf of California, trying to forget all the dams that block its way.

We are back at our campsite after hiking through the spectacular lower gorge of Deer Creek. Dinner is relaxed as the evening drops its soothing cover of cool darkness. As we roll out the sleeping bags, someone notices a tiny light, high on the steep, rocky trail that leads down to the campsite. Looks like we may have late visitors. We watch as the light wavers, then goes out, and then on again. Then it's gone. There must be someone there who has either decided to stop or is in trouble. It's a big boulder field up there with no logical place to camp and not a drop of water.

We must go up that trail and find out if there's a problem. Randy, Jack and I gather up canteens of water, first aid and flashlights and start up the rocky slope. Even with three flashlights we lose the trail in several spots. As I put my hand on the still warm boulders, I wonder if our slithering, pink friends are close by. We are over halfway to the top when our lights suddenly focus on a person huddled in the midst of the rocks and boulders. A middle-aged man is sitting there in the dark, his water gone. He is unable to walk because of severe leg cramps brought on by dehydration. He promptly drains one of our canteens and tells us that he has come thirteen miles from Indian Hollow and, although he often hikes alone in the Canyon and knows its danger, he did not expect such unusually hot temperatures this late in the year.

He tries to get up, but his legs are not working well. I suggest that Randy carry his pack, but he is very proud and stubborn. Finally, after more attempts to walk, he agrees to the idea. We make our way very slowly down the trail, picking our way between the dark rocks, helping the gentleman along without being too solicitous. Slow going, but we finally reach our campsite where we help him set up camp, fix some soup, give him vitamins and minerals to help replace those lost in dehydration and then, when we are sure that he is settled for the night, we crawl into our own bags.

It's been a long day and it's a good feeling to know that we were here and just happened to spot that tiny light on the hill. I'm finally dozing off when a sharp sting on my back sends me to my feet. I grab the culprit instantly and throw it on the tarp, but can't really identify it by flashlight. In spite of complaints, I get no sympathy from the half-asleep bodies lying nearby. One even had the nerve to say, "It's only a spider. Go back to sleep." So I did.

THIRD DAY

In the morning light I investigate the insect I squashed last night and it looks suspiciously like a scorpion. Randy gets his magnifying glass and, sure enough, it is. He consults the first-aid book and relates all the dire effects of a scorpion sting and what to do. "Keep the patient still and quiet for eight hours" is one suggestion. All of which I've just finished doing. We read on, but the only flaw in this scenario is that I feel fine and most of all I'm hungry. Once again we do our own diagnosis and decide that either I'm immune to scorpion venom, which I doubt, or that this was an immature

Scorpion

22

or malfunctioning one without much poison in its sting. We'll never know, of course, but I do know that I will never again break the cardinal rule of the desert by rolling out my sleeping bag before I'm ready to get into it.

With insects taken care of, it's time to check on our friend under the trees. He seems to be doing okay except for severe cramps in his fingers. We offer to stay another night or walk out with him, but he is determined to go on to Kanab Creek as part o his solo, ten-day trip. Fortunately he will have plenty of water along the way. I'm sure he feels embarrassed about all the fuss so we say our goodbyes and wish him luck. Randy will stay awhile in camp to see if he's all right, but there's nothing more we can do. It would have been nice if he'd just said "thank you."

Back up the steep rocks and through Surprise Valley again, on our way to Thunder River. Still very hot. But now I can see what the place looks like. Pretty bleak and empty with absolutely no shade. A large, fuzzy, black tarantula marches across the trail. You'd think he'd be unbearably hot in that black fur coat and leggings. Cynthia and Jack are tired and we are all wilting from the heat. It's easy walking, but for those new to the desert I'm sure this particular land-scape doesn't have much appeal.

Just about the time that spirits have drooped low, we hear a distant roar and, as we drop over the next hill, we are all astonished to see in the dry, desolate cliff ahead a tremendous waterfall coming right out of the rock wall. Thunder Falls! What an amazing sight!

With new energy, we wind our way down the trail, with the water always in view, and then the green world emerges. Cottonwood trees, lush vegetation and rocks covered with mosses and maidenhair fern line the valley, all created by the precious water of Thunder Falls, which drains a large part of the Kaibab Plateau, way up beyond the North Rim. This also is what makes the Canyon so special — the astonishing contrasts between the dryness and lushness, all within a day's walk.

Thunder River itself is only half a mile long and drains into Tapeats Creek, where we will camp tonight. This is a sparkling stream quite deep and wide, fringed by the usual welcome cottonwoods, with lovely camping spots. Tomorrow we'll explore upper Tapeats, but now we dump the heavy packs and go back up the trail to sit under the spray of Thunder Falls. It's an absolute paradise as the water roars past us and sends its cool veils of water showering over our hot bodies.

We are camped in a green world tonight, with softly fluttering cottonwoods overhead, the refreshing sound of the creek in our ears, nobody to rescue in the dark of the night and hopefully no scorpions in our sleeping bags. All seems well with our little world in the bottom of the Grand Canyon of Arizona.

FOURTH DAY

This is a day at camp and it means we spread out our belongings, figure out where we put the wrong things in the various pockets of our pack, nibble on gorp, lie on the tarp and then, when all those pressing items are resolved, we decide it's time to explore.

Walking upstream along Tapeats Creek is delightful! The stream meanders through the red cliffs fringed by the lush green of water-loving vegetation. As we round a bend of the creek we are greeted by a deep, enticing pool which is

Collared Lizard

immediately filled with naked, carefree bodies shouting and experiencing the sheer joy of cool, jade-green water and a soft cascading waterfall. The dry heat of Surprise Valley is long forgotten as Cynthia and Jack dive down deep into that jewel of a pool. I feel, for the moment at least, no remorse in having persuaded them to come to the Canyon with us.

We dry out on the hot, red rocks and then repeat the whole procedure over and over again, with more hiking along the creek, more pools and warm rocks to lie upon while the desert breeze evaporates the silver droplets on our tan skin. A collared lizard from a nearby rock, dressed in its formal green vest, watches these strange creatures, shakes its head, and slips away to its more reasonable world.

A good day for all and another mellow night. Once again I contemplate the contrasts of the desert. Without the heat, the thirst, the prickly, scratchy bleakness of places like Surprise Valley, we'd never appreciate this oasis in the same way. The heavy pack, the sore toes, the aching head, the complaining muscles, and then the cool, soothing water with the breeze rustling and the green, cottonwood leaves and the lacy, tamarisk boughs. The agony and the ecstasy is what it is all about.

Our Canyon threesome—Randy, Murray and I—likes to finish a trip with the last night spent partway to the rim, with an overview of where we have been and the opportunity for the sunset to put on its evening performance. So the plan is to leave Thunder Falls late in the afternoon, bring up all the water we can carry, and have a dry camp in Surprise Valley for our final night. But this morning we'll walk down Tapeats Creek to the Colorado River for another look at the deep, fast flowing water which is still carving the Grand Canyon.

Afternoon shadows are lengthening as we fill our water bottles with the cold, clear water which falls in silver strands from Thunder Falls. It's hard to leave the bliss of moist, green vegetation and the sound of water filling every nook. We look back longingly as we struggle up the steep trail loaded with water, leaving that verdant fairyland behind. As we enter the dry, hot ridge looking down into Surprise Valley, we take one last look at the phenomena of that gigantic water spout, shooting out of the red wall of the Canyon.

Our campsite is a high point with long views. Just the way we like it. The sun is slowly sinking and the evening color show is about to begin. We are not disappointed, as the molten gold turns to the scarlet red of hot iron. The promontories, citadels and buttes absorb the brilliant hues until one feels aglow with the excitement of it all. At last it begins to fade, perspective collapses and there is no perception of distance, just a violet haze over all.

We go about the chores of the evening, feeling relaxed and mellow. Our last night. The threesome feels sad, but I sense that Cynthia and Jack are glad to see it come to an end. Perhaps we planned too ambitious a trip for their first introduction to the Canyon. It's better to ease into this world more gradually, down the South Kaibab or Bright Angel trails, where civilization is closer and security can be found more easily. Affection and addiction for the Grand Canyon don't usually happen overnight. We addicts have forgotten, I'm afraid.

SIXTH DAY

A warm morning again, even though it's very early. We always like to get the ascent of the Redwall out of the way before the temperature soars. Those hot, solar rays bounce right off the dark, red rocks and cliffs onto one's vulnerable and defenseless skin. I still haven't decided if it's cooler to take off as much as possible or follow the phi losophy of an Israeli hiking friend, who claims that he is always cooler with a loose-fitting, long-sleeved shirt and long pants. That worked for him in the deserts of the Near East and when he backpacked this same route with us the following year, but so far I'm not convinced. I like the freedom of as few clothes as possible, with a wet shirt and hat if there's surplus water available.

And so it's up and up and up—always, at the end of a Canyon trip. Cynthia and Jack are racing ahead, glad to get out of this gigantic hole in the earth, but the three of us are making it last a little longer. Lunch among the juniper trees with a short siesta in the shade of their fragrant boughs. Not much further to go and I still have plenty of Thunder Falls' water. No point in hauling it up to the rim, so I relish in the luxury of pouring it over my head, feeling like I've performed a criminal act. Water is so precious in the desert and backpackers' lives are controlled by this treasured resource.

We are close to the rim as we stop often to look back, re-membering that first, scary day in Surprise Valley, and also wondering if the man we found that night has made it safely to Kanab Creek.

The car is waiting for us at Monument Point, where we left it six days ago. As the afternoon begins to get very cool, we take the final pictures, pop open the cans of beer, and, as we bounce along the twenty miles of dirt road back to the main highway of the North Rim, we finally realize that the trip is over.

CHAPTER 3

Silence and Isolation

Kanab Creek • October 1980

Fall is nearly over in the Colorado mountains. A few golden leaves still hang on the nearly bare branches, but winter is in the air. The hunters are taking over the high country, so it's time to leave for the desert. Our threesome is looking for a real wilderness adventure. The western end of the Grand Canyon is still relatively unknown and very beautiful, so we have chosen Kanab Creek for a ten-day October trip.

Thirty miles of dirt road from the North Rim highway and we arrive at Sowats Point, where the trailhead begins our twenty-five mile trip to the Colorado River. We will camp tonight on this isolated promontory, high on the rim, with expansive vistas down into the twisting sinuosities of Indian Hollow and Jumpup Canyon. It's late afternoon as that mystical, golden luster touches every rock and bush. Randy walks out to a distant viewpoint and I follow, as Murray explores other areas.

The feeling is very different in this wide open western end of the Canyon. Very few hike here, and there is a wonderful, wild sensation all around. As I return to the car I hear Murray calling some unintelligible warning, which turns out to be about a large, well-camouflaged rattler near where we'll camp. Not the small, pinkish and shy Canyon rattler, but more like the real western diamondback. The evening fortunately has turned quite cool, so he or she is curled up, hopefully quite comatose for the night.

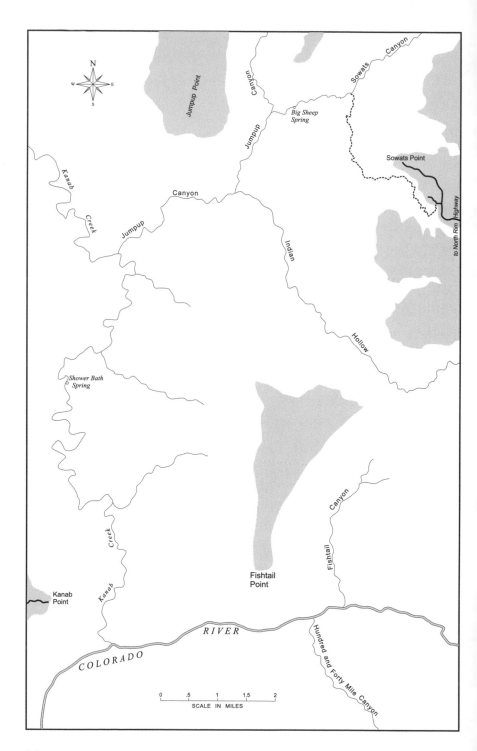

N
W E
S

Jumpup Point

Jumpup Canyon

Big Sheep Spring

Sowats Canyon

Sowats Point

Kanab Creek

Jumpup Canyon

Jumpup

Indian

Hollow

to North Rim Highway

Shower Bath Spring

Fishtail Canyon

Fishtail

Kanab Creek

Kanab Point

Fishtail Point

RIVER

COLORADO

Hundred and Forty Mile Canyon

0   .5   1   1.5   2
SCALE IN MILES

30

The day dawns fair and warm. A new adventure is about to begin. Ten days. Twenty-five miles to the river through unknown territory. The last zipper is closed on the pack and, with the usual grunts and groans, I lift my heavy house onto my back. Murray and I start down toward Sowats Canyon, leaving fleet-footed Randy to close up the car. The trail winds its way through grey-green sage and golden rabbitbrush, interspersed with large, chalk-white, limestone boulders. Ahead is a lone stand of very green cottonwoods, indicating a hidden spring in this very dry landscape. It's the usual good walking along the Esplanade among round, mushroom-shaped rocks, before dropping into the waterless creekbed.

Our lunch spot will be Big Sheep Spring, where we understand there is water. Also, there should be pictographs near the spring. We look carefully in all directions with no luck. Randy climbs up some red slickrock, still hunting, as Murray and I settle down for lunch by the tiny stream. We hear Randy call, a rather embarrassed call, saying he's stuck and can't get down. Murray clambers up the slickrock, gets a good foothold and is able to stretch up high enough to make a platform with one hand for Randy to step on and work his way down. Sometimes it's hard to remember that what goes up must come down. As I return to my interrupted lunch, I look around and, there on a wall right behind me, are the pictographs! Six well-preserved hand prints, just my size, two unusual figures, and a sheep. Big Sheep Spring—did the Anasazis see a mountain sheep here or were they just doodling on a lazy afternoon centuries ago?

We continue along the creekbed where our friendly, little stream suddenly disappears. Sad to leave a water source.

It's always a welcome companion and the absence of water makes a trip more serious, depending on the location of the next supply.

Jumpup Canyon now, named appropriately because the only way out in a flash flood is up—only problem being that the surrounding walls are a good 200 feet high. Jumpup is a spectacular, narrow slit through the Redwall, with Indian Hollow coming in from the southeast. We are walking in a dry streambed through a canyon that winds and turns through niches less than six feet wide in places. The azure blue sky high up in the slash between the cliffs reassures us, since this is not the place to be in a heavy rain and flood. The polished walls are sculptured into lovely, convoluted art forms, sometimes in deep blue shadow, and then splashed with dazzling sunshine.

We walk, topo map in hand, trying to keep track of the dozens of sinuosities in order to have some idea of how far we've gone. The walking surface is covered with round river rocks and it's hard on the ankles as we make our way down the gently sloping, dry creekbed. A bit weary by now, and we consider camping where Indian Hollow comes in, that is, until we get there. The sun is no longer in this deep ravine and Indian Hollow is a jumble of rocks in a spooky dark recess. Hardly a welcoming campsite. Our only alternative is to go on a few miles to the confluence of Kanab Creek, although we understand that water begins two miles downstream from there. But our canteens of water are holding out well and it's cool hiking, so onward to Kanab.

The confluence is a welcome, wide area and, beautiful as Jumpup was, it's good to be able to see out again. The sun has set and we hurry to set up camp and fix dinner before the light is totally gone. It's been a long but wonderful day.

Bright sun pours over the cliff walls as we pack up for the next stint towards the river. The Redwall Formation is deeper in the western Grand Canyon than further upriver and is absolutely one of the most scenic parts we have been in yet. The walls must be close to 1,000 feet high. We are tiny dots at the bottom of this grandeur. The water has appeared and the reds and pinks are reflected in the winding, clear stream. We crisscross back and forth through the water, finally leaving it once again to enter a very hot, higher environment. The sun is directly overhead and there is hardly a breath of wind as we make our way, shortcutting a loop in the creek, through cacti, prickly bushes and hot, red soil.

We drop down to the creek once more, and there is the most amazing sight! On a gigantic rock overhang is a tremendous growth of maidenhair fern and heavy, wet vegetation, dotted with brilliant, red monkeyflowers, extending twenty feet out from the wall. It's like a gargantuan, green sponge hanging there with silvery strands of water pouring out of it. We are convinced we have reached paradise for sure as we stand under the delicate cascade of water. Heads bend back and water slips down parched throats, pours over hot backs and slithers down tummies. We yell and holler, lacking adjectives to express our ecstasy.

Monkeyflower

Finally we fill the water bottles with the sparkling threads of water and reluctantly say good-bye to this sublime fairy-land. In 1872 Frederick Dellenbaugh discovered this same spot as he made his way out of the Canyon at the end of the second Powell river expedition. He named it "Shower Bath Spring." We did not encounter the local residents he de-scribed as infesting the place — tarantulas, scorpions, rattle-snakes and gila monsters!

The trail begins to get more difficult, with large boulders blocking our way. Deep pools are tucked in among the rocks and rubble, and we detour many times looking for the easi-est way through this maze. We wade through the small pools and the cool water feels good oozing from my boots. The Canyon is becoming narrower, with towering cliffs on either side and the deepest blue sky above that one can imagine. Cattails grow alongside the pools, with lush green plants trailing off the lower cliffs, sustained by the life-giving water. It's been a picture-book hike, with that incredi-ble surprise — the green, dripping sponge. Camp is made in a flat, sandy spot near the stream as the late sun finally leaves us in shadow and works its way up the perpendicular, pink cliffs that reach to the sky.

THIRD DAY

The excellent weather continues, although the lower we get, the hotter. Kanab Creek twists and turns between big boulders and deep pools, and we continue to search for the best way through the puzzle. Such a rugged canyon, with unscalable walls on both sides that seem to close in behind and before us. And yet the feeling is not op-pressive since the chattering creek and cheerful vegetation are always with us. The canyon is so deep that shade is always just around the comer. But finding a campsite is not so easy. At last we find a place large enough for three sleeping bags. Our night sky is a long, ebony slot above. The stars within it sparkle down on us as we end another day in Kanab Creek Canyon.

FOURTH DAY

Only a short hike to the river today. The creekbed widens and a few tamarisks appear on the sandbars. We arrive at our friend, the Colorado River, still flowing swiftly on its way down to Lava Falls and then on to Lake Mead. A raft, far on the other side, is our first glimpse of other Homo sapiens since we left the highway five days ago. It's gone in an instant and we inspect our new home. Shopping for a homesite here is a breeze—white sand, large, shady trees and bushes, quiet, warm Kanab Creek beside us and the majestic Colorado in front. The large, green tarp goes up for shade, the ropes are hung for the food bags, essentials are arranged, lunch is eaten, and now it's time for play.

Kanab Creek is beckoning. Its water is clear, cool and deliciously refreshing as we skinny dip, dance and frolic, sending a spray of jewels into the air. Then back to our Robinson Crusoe home under the tarp, our backs resting against propped-up packs, toes wriggling in the sand and time no longer part of our life. The river goes by, a fly lazily buzzes around my head, eyelids begin to droop. Randy is already sound asleep, his paperback book lying unopened in the sand.

The ending of each day in the Canyon is always special. The sun gets lower, the colors become dramatic as the reds and oranges climb up the cliffs, leaving deep, purple shadows below. Then only the tops of the jagged pinnacles are touched with fire, and finally the show is over.

The bats arrive, swooping and diving for their daily insect fare as our cheese soup bubbles away on the little stove. A gourmet treat when poured over instant mashed potatoes, with a side of rehydrated fresh spinach and a chocolate bar for desert. What could possibly be better? The stars are appearing faster than I can count in the blue-black sky above us. All is perfection on this little beach.

FIFTH DAY

The cloudless days go on. No packs to put on today. No hurry, no destination—a day to explore, play in the water, write in my journal, a day to be in one of the world's dwindling, wild and natural, hidden places.

A hike along the river, lunch on the warm sand, watching the somewhat muddy water flow by. There's a quietness about the river here with no rapids to break the stillness. A raft goes by with several kayakers alongside. They don't even know we're here. Back at camp, we discover that clear Kanab Creek has been pushed back up its canyon by the rising Colorado. It's been hot in the cities and the human robots that control Glen Canyon Dam are releasing more water to generate power for Southwestern air conditioners, hairdryers and television sets.

Our last night at our beachfront hotel with the green tarp. We will start up tomorrow, twenty-five miles back to Sowats Point. Someday it would be fun to go back east along the river to Deer Creek and out through Surprise Valley. Another idea to dream about. But this trip has been superb. We have not met a single person on the "trail." The river boat people go by quickly, as though it were a dream.

We watch the rose and golden lights bounce off the burnished surface of the Colorado. Still a great river, though tamed by the dam. It flows 1,400 miles from its source in the high mountains near Granby, Colorado, to the Gulf of California. By the time it reaches there no water is left, since agricultural projects, cities, and industries have taken such greedy gulps. All the tributaries, including the San Juan, the Green, the Yampa, the Little Colorado, the Gunnison, and the Dirty Devil, which are rivers in their own right, drain into the Colorado. So all these man-made demands are draining an entire river system. I try not to think of all this as I watch the colors fade and the evening blues and mauves fill the canyon. Dinner is finished, the food bags are hung high on a line stretched between the tamarisks, and another day ends.

I am awakened out of a deep slumber by a noisy, unidentified sound. I sit up and flash my light over the hanging food bags. Our large, light blue bag looks very strange. It seems to have acquired a peculiar, furry thing around it. I wake up Murray just as the light encounters two flashing, amber eyes peering from around the bag. A ringtail cat has discovered the possibilities of a change of diet. We throw some sand at him and he jumps off the bag, followed by a huge, black and white ringed tail almost as long as his body. We settle down once more, only to hear the same telltale sounds of little, sharp claws digging into the bag. Back again, gracefully curled around it, daring us to frighten him away. But lovely as he is, protecting our food is critical and

Ringtail

besides, human edibles wouldn't be good for him anyway. Once more we send him away and this time we light the candle lantern and put it under the bags in the sand, hopefully to discourage him and to also provide a better view. It works and the night continues uneventfully, without our nocturnal visitor.

SIXTH DAY

The food bag is inspected. Nothing is missing, but it is riddled with tiny holes where our friend dug in his sharp claws. What a delightful treat to see Mr. Ringtail, even though it was in the middle of the night.

We reluctantly pack up, take down our green, nylon roof, pick up every tiny bit of human trash, smooth out the sand where we've left large imprints, load our packs on once again, say our farewells to this storybook spot, and start up the canyon. Back to the climbing, boulder after boulder, stretching every muscle to find a foothold and handhold, up one side and down the other, always with the cumbersome load fastened to one's back. We detour around rock giants, with hidden pools too deep to wade, retracing our steps, looking for the magic carpet out of this collection of rocks. Charming little gardens where the water is shallow appear now and then and provide us with places to sit and snack and have short siestas. High walls again surround us and offer cooling shadows. Kanab Creek is a huge gorge. This stream is the only tributary of the Colorado River to have cut through the high plateau from sources to the north.

Again the search for a level place big enough to put three sleeping bags for the night. It's a tight spot, but we'll fit. There is a small side canyon just below us, filled with jungle-like greenery, red monkeyflowers and mossy, fluorescent green rocks. Randy can never resist seeing what's up a narrow corridor and promptly takes off up the tiny canyon. We are in the deepest part of the gorge now and darkness arrives early in that sliver of sky overhead.

SEVENTH DAY

Gradually we are leaving the boulder-laden streambed. The walls, though, seem to be getting higher, covered with black desert varnish, with trailing green vegetation tucked into every niche and anchored to each ledge. The "trail" follows bends in the streambed, occasional detours up and over dry hillocks filled with cacti and dried, tan grasses, and then down again to the moist world of water. A lovely walk for sure.

The perfect fall weather continues. Still no sign of humans. Just the three of us hiking along, quiet much of the time, often spread out on the trail along the way, each absorbing the grandeur and beauty, stopping and sharing when we see something special. Through the years we've reached this comfortable companionship and, as the days go by in each trip, we find we are really in tune with nature and life is definitely in balance. If only we could hang onto this feeling when life in that other world gets hectic and crazy.

We are now in the deepest part of the Redwall Formation. The cliff walls go up and up, reaching towards the cobalt sky, leaving us tiny humans gawking upwards, trying to grasp, intellectually, how high we are looking.

October coolness is creeping over the land as the elevation increases. The sun sets very early, reminding us that winter will be just around the corner when we return to the Colorado mountains. But I won't think about that now. I want to relish each moment of these last few days and will file them away in my memory to be pulled out when life needs a good lift.

EIGHT DAY

Today we'll be doing the twists and turns of Jumpup Canyon. The last little running water is left behind as we reach the rocky, dry streambed. Never have I seen so many round rocks, each one an invitation to twist an ankle. The canyon is becoming narrower with each step. We notice that the blue sky has begun to get very grey and hurry instinctively, with flash floods in the back of our minds. The dark entrance to Indian Hollow is passed, as we try once more to count the sinuosities on our topo map, now and then glancing at the sliver of grey overhead. As I hurry along on the rocky corridor I am suddenly flat on my back, trapped by my pack like a turtle wrong side up! No harm done, but I need Murray's helping hand to get out of my predicament. Something about "haste makes waste" runs through my head and I slow down.

At last this narrow world opens up and we are free! We continue on until the trickle of water in the creekbed starts once more. We find a lovely, open camping place with a large boulder for a table, a smooth, sandy floor, and away from the danger of flash floods.

The sky is lightly overcast but we decide "no tents tonight" and, after a leisurely supper and a short session with my journal, we settle in. Tomorrow will be a short climb up and out of Sowats Canyon to the friendly Esplanade.

NINTH DAY

Late and lazy breakfast this morning. No rush at all. Murray and I put on our much lighter packs and take off, leaving Randy to do the final smoothing out of our tracks on the canyon floor and to follow at his leisure. Back to Big Sheep Spring and the gentle stream, where we weigh down the packs again with water for our dry camp tonight.

The sun has appeared as we begin the easy climb out to the Esplanade, where we will have our final camp. One last look down, with all those good memories, and we stride out over the smooth, red dirt. The long vistas are with us again and it is a great sensation to look out in every direction in a world of space. Plenty of campsites here in this piñon and juniper woodland, where each tree and bush is spaced far apart, protecting its own underground water supply.

There are suspicious, dark clouds building up on the horizon, so for the first time, up go the tents. At least we didn't carry them for nothing. The last night. We sit among the aromatic junipers, imagining how the Indians used their shaggy bark for ropes, roofing and even diapers for their babies. The piñons provided sweet pine nuts, so a woodland such as this must have been important to them. It's important to me, but for other reasons. Most of all, how fortunate we are to have these irreplaceable lands protected by National Park designation. How easily they could have slipped away to development, roads, and man-made desecration. Without our National Parks and designated Wilderness areas, it would soon be impossible to be alone with nature without signs of man's tampering.

TENTH DAY

Sun and clouds fill the immense sky this morning. Randy laughs as I go almost headfirst down into my pack, hunting for the last breakfast meal. The orderly system of the first few days has completely disintegrated and I can't find anything. My house is a mess!

Murray and I start out first, leaving Randy to "soak up a little more of the Esplanade," as he describes it. We pass the familiar, lush stand of cottonwoods and the sharp, white limestone rocks. The ground cover is thick around the trees, with four-wing saltbush, golden rabbitbrush, and prickly pear cacti poking their spiny leaves up here and there. The clouds are getting thicker and darker and we speed up a bit as sheets of rain obscure the distant cliffs to the west. Then a big cloud opens up over Jumpup Canyon, leaving the mesas shining and wet. We feel lucky being here, rather than deep in that narrow chasm. Dark, sinister clouds are rolling in, but only a few sprinkles here so far as we continue the climb up to that far-away rim. Randy may soak up more than the

Esplanade if he doesn't hurry.

Soon we can just make out the van parked on the top, looking like a small, brown and tan box and, just about the time we reach our box, the rain begins. In go the packs, we slam the door and congratulate ourselves on our good timing. We'll start the car and be ready to leave the minute Randy arrives, since the thirty miles of dirt, rutted road to the highway can become impassable with heavy rains. I step on the starter and nothing happens!

Randy arrives and tries his skills, with no luck. Thirty minutes pass. The rain stops. Randy and Murray try again to figure out the problem. We discuss our situation. We can all backpack out the thirty miles, which would take nearly three days, or one person could go — Randy, no doubt — with a light pack, spend one night and hitchhike from the main highway to the North Rim Village for help. Of course if the rain should turn to snow, we'd really be in trouble. Cars have been known to have spent the winter at some of these deserted trailheads. Looks like we'll be staying here awhile, so I take out a couple of folding chairs, some crackers and cheese, and decide to make myself comfortable.

Randy tries once more to start the van and, lo and behold, a spark ignites and it's going! I grab the chairs, jump into the back, while Randy keeps his foot on the accelerator and we let out whoops and hollers as we leave Sowats Point. And so a wonderful trip ends on a happy note.

CHAPTER 4

Desert and River

Tanner to Grandview • April 1981

FIRST DAY

Under the cool and cloudy skies our spring, ten-day trip begins at Lipan Point near Desert View on the eastern end of the South Rim. Murray, Randy and I are joined by Randy's friend Al whom he first met in the Grand Canyon at his camping spot near Clear Creek. Murray and I drop below the rim of the Tanner Trailhead, leaving the boys to shuttle cars and follow later. Our fifty-pound packs weigh down each careful step as we gingerly pick our way down, down the rocky trail.

Here the Canyon is quite open and the whole panorama spreads out below us, with the wide expanse of river nine miles below, its green borders of vegetation beckoning us. Mist hangs over the high rock spires and slips down into the gorges, leaving subtle roses and lavenders coloring the cliffs. Slowly it lifts as the sun begins to break through, turning towers and pinnacles into a fairyland of gold. Piñon and juniper trees, after last night's rain, give off a heady fragrance.

The trail continues steep and rough where just one rock could turn underfoot and send you flat on your face or behind. We stop now and then just to observe this marvel called the Grand Canyon spread out before us. Finally, after about a mile of rough scrambling, we land on a rocky ridge with spectacular views down Seventyfive Mile Canyon, west

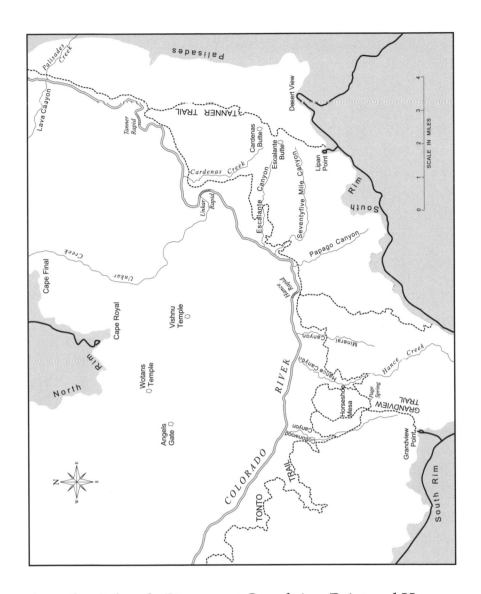

along the Colorado River, past Grandview Point and Horseshoe Mesa, into the vast, hazy distance beyond.

The trail levels off, with gentle ups and downs over the
dark red remains of the Supai Formation. We skirt two
buttes—Escalante, named for the famous pioneer priest, and
Cardenas, honoring the Spanish explorer.

High above on the South Rim we can see the tall, round tower of Desert View, where the human ants scurry to and from their cars and buses to shop for souvenirs and perhaps, in between, take a quick glance into one of the wonders of the world lying below them in all its glory.

Piñons and juniper trees dot the landscape, with only a few flowers because of the drought this spring, but every now and then scarlet Indian paintbrush and white phlox surprise us along the way. A stop to fix a pack and bandage a toe before a blister begins and then on again after measured sips of precious water. Nine dry miles and all we have to drink is on our backs. As we reach a saddle, we can see our eventual destination far below, where the Colorado River serpentines around Unkar and Tanner rapids and the eastern Palisades. The blue-green water has turned to muddy brown after a badly needed recent rain.

Now down the Redwall, always a steep and tricky series of switchbacks, with the noonday sun beating down. We seek out a lone juniper tree for shade as we lunch on sardines and hard-boiled eggs. Such luxuries are only for the first day, with maybe an orange or apple, and then it's dried food for the remainder of the trip. Each time we try to figure out ways to lighten our packs, with little success, so on they go again, miserable but essential.

We are over halfway but the end seems a million miles off as the heat intensifies over the red Dox Sandstone. But moving feet can cover distances in an amazing way and the sight of green willows and tamarisks in the distance speeds up those faithful feet. I go faster and faster down Tanner Wash, that oven of a dry streambed. Murray describes me as a horse headed for the barn. But I know that there's cold, forty-five-degree water just waiting for soaking heads and

Spotted Ground Squirrel

toes at the end of the road and I'm on my way!

Ah, ecstasy! Our old campsite under an aged mesquite tree is waiting for us, as Tanner Rapids greets us with its usual roar. Those abominable fifty pounds are finally dumped off our backs and my sore, hot toes dangle in the fast-flowing river. It's now 3:25 P.M. and we purify the murky river water in our plastic bottles, renew our acquaintances with the beautiful surrounding cliffs and say hello to the ubiquitous and curious lizards who will share our site. The temperature is ninety degrees and we find ourselves involved with trivia. The rhythm of civilization still is in control of our time clocks. We wait for Randy and Al. We hang our food bags to outwit the night residents as a day critter, a squirrel, already has found its way into the granola.

The boys arrive at 7:00 P.M. and we dine together on the warm sand of Tanner Beach. The almost full moon is lighting up our living room and the temperature has dropped to an ideal seventy degrees. Jupiter and Saturn are above us, competing with the light of the moon. A bat whirls by on silent wings. Al is in his yellow, down cocoon and Randy writes in his journal by candle lantern. Stretching out on my bag in the soft sand, watching the moonbeams dance on the high cliffs, is an almost instant prescription for sleep.

A brilliant, blue, desert morning. The heat is already penetrating through the tiny leaves of the mesquite tree as we munch on granola and dried fruit. This is to be a lazy day with only four miles to go later in the day, eastward upstream, to Palisade Creek. We spend the morning on the sandy shore in the shade of the willows. A large, spotted lizard with bulging eyes sits on a log surveying this motley group. Al and Randy are reading, with Murray content simply to watch the water go by. A couple of other hikers arrive to share our shade. A peaceful scene until a rattler quietly slithers across the sand into the bushes. He ignores us, finds a soft spot under the willows, stretches luxuriously and then gracefully winds him or herself into a large round mass, puts its head down on the smooth, pink skin and promptly goes to sleep.

More hikers are arriving so it's time to leave and head upriver for more privacy. Many people hike down the Tanner, spend the night, and go back up the next morning. Quick trips for those in a hurry. So we leave our friend, the old mesquite tree, cross the dry creekbed and climb up the trail, high above the river, over the dark red rocks which are giving off enough solar heat to power a city. Al takes a detour and almost finds himself trapped on a shaley slope, but eventually joins us as we drop down to the beach below the stately Palisades.

Our favorite spot is occupied by a river group running the dories, the wooden boats which somewhat resemble those Major Powell and his group used on the first trip to explore the Grand Canyon. We visit with the boat people, but the sight of their cold beer, and no offers, sends us onward. Climbing over some warm rocks finds us taking a sudden detour as a pink rattler blocks our way. As we are about to settle down on the sandy shoreline, another rattler cruises by. Never have we seen so many snakes in one day! But this is their home and we are but intruders, so we observe them with respect and appreciate their tolerance of us.

Camp is set up on the smooth, white beach and, without a tree in sight, rigging a line to hold our food bags becomes a challenge, but with long pieces of driftwood and a little ingenuity it's accomplished, while tiny, bright eyes watch from every rock in disappointment.

THIRD DAY

A layover day at camp with time to explore, wash hair and just enjoy walking around without a pack. Randy goes birding and Murray and I walk up to the abandoned copper mine at Lava Canyon. The remains of an old cabin still stand, with rotting logs slowly becoming part of the desert environment. What an isolated and hard life those early miners lived in their quest for riches. We poke our heads into the old mine with not much enthusiasm for going further into its dark recesses.

The Canyon is wide where we are camping. Wonderful long beaches with the water lapping quietly along the shore. No rapids roaring in our ears, as night slips down over our little world. A dinner of chili beans, cabbage and yogurt drops, all products of my handy dehydrator, which prepares them at home in Old Snowmass. A leisurely evening as the candle lanterns cast their cheerful rays over the sand. Cool breezes drift over the water, the stars are in their proper places and all is well in the bottom of the Grand Canyon.

I am rudely awakened by rain on my nose. But, suspecting that the weather might change, we had put up the tents last night and hardly lose ten winks of sleep as we move quickly into them. Morning comes with the crowing of a rooster who bears a strong resemblance to Randy. He'd refused to put up his tent and is sitting, draped with a tarp, quite damp and ready to move on.

We pack up our soggy stuff, gulp down oatmeal, and take off under sodden skies back westward, downriver, past our Tanner campsite, to Unkar Rapids. As we come down off the high, red hillside the sky turns black and threatening, the wind and rain let loose. A wonderful wild storm with thunder and lightning bouncing back and forth over the cliffs. A welcome, large, rock overhang is right ahead for us to huddle under and watch the thirsty land absorb the life-giving drops of water.

Before we reach Unkar the rain ends, leaving the world washed and refreshed. It's a lovely hike over the red, rolling hills, high above the brown river. We drop down to the shore in search of a campsite as the clouds return.

Tonight even Randy decides in favor of a tent. In our early trips to the Canyon we carried only tarp, but after some horrendous downpours we decided the extra weight of a tent was worth the pleasure of staying dry. It seems though now the drought has broken, as the steady patter of rain on the nylon roof sends me quickly to dreamland.

FIFTH DAY

Today we must climb up and over the red rock "Cockscomb" which separates Unkar from Escalante Canyon. Sunshine again, but cool breezes as we start the climb. Spectacular views from the towering walls above Unkar Rapids and the broad delta where Indian ruins were excavated in 1967. With plenty of water and flat land for growing crops, it was a logical place for an Anasazi community centuries ago. We lunch high on the Cockscomb, with panoramic views spread out below us, stretch out over the warm rocks, munching on dried pineapple without a care in the world. Time slips by.

Reality takes over when we remember that a rough trail is ahead, with a long dry trip past Escalante and up to and back down the deep slash of Seventyfive Mile Canyon. In fact there really isn't a trail here. A few years ago Randy, on a solo trip, followed a misplaced cairn and mistakenly dropped into a side canyon, discovered he was lost and nearly out of water on an extremely hot day. Trying to remain calm, he sat quietly and suddenly spied a bird, which kept coming to the same spot below him over and over. He went down and discovered a damp spot of sand where he could depress a teaspoon and fill it with precious water. Though it was a long process to fill a canteen, his hopes rose and he retraced his steps back up to the right route and all was well.

So up to the head of Seventyfive Mile Canyon and down its very dry and rocky streambed, with many twists and turns until the river appears. A small beach awaits us, just right for camping, and it's all ours. Happy Easter, everyone!

With the prospect of a long day of hiking awaiting us, we get an early start for Hance Canyon. To start the day off, we must climb hand over hand up the rock outcropping of Papago Canyon, up chimneys where our packs seem to always manage to get caught on uncooperative rocks.

Halfway up, a curious chuckwalla, a large, prehistoric-looking lizard, comes closer to us than he intended and then retreats to a narrow cleft, where he puffs himself up, out of harm's way.

As we hang high over the river, I realize that to get down the other side I must somehow negotiate this frightening array of rocks and scree which seems to drop off into nowhere. Even without a heavy pack it wouldn't be fun, but now I must balance this monster on my back as I slide and

Chuckwalla

stumble my way down towards Hance Beach. My knees are trembling, my mouth is dry, but at last the worst is over and I look back smugly as Murray picks and slips his way down the treacherous chute.

A well-earned lunch on the beach at Hance Rapid and then up over sand dunes to the Tonto Trail, that long route stretching for many miles above the Inner Gorge. Wet hats and scarves keep us tolerably cool as the temperature soars. Seven miles to go this afternoon. The trail seems endless, with one loop after another, on and on under the blistering sun. Just when I have begun to think that one more loop will about finish me, my hot head and aching toes rejoice as I realize we have reached Hance Creek.

Happy day, the burros are gone! With all the controversy about removing them, it's great to have them out of the Canyon. This was not their natural home and the damage to the natural vegetation, which is necessary to support the native wildlife, the pollution of the streams and the general mess they left are a few of the reasons the Park Service decided to remove them. Hopefully they are all happy elsewhere.

Four tired hikers tonight, as we spread out our bags, watch the moon filter through the cottonwood trees, and listen to the frogs and toads tune up for their nightly serenade.

SEVENTH DAY

Cottonwood Canyon, just west of Horseshoe Mesa, is our destination for today, but we are faced with the never-ending loops of the long trail along the Tonto Platform. The land is bleak, but lovely in its bleakness, with sudden surprises of brilliant, pink hedgehog cacti appearing between the blackbush. As I put one foot after the other I become almost automated as the miles are covered. Seems as though I could go on forever, but Murray breaks the spell and suggests lunch. Suddenly, my pack is off and I'm hungry! Angel's Gate, that impressive monolith across the river, is before us, surrounded by a kaleidoscope of pinks, blues and purples, with a tiny snatch of brown river far below us. To think it was only yesterday that we sat and cooled our sore toes in that same river.

We find a perfect campsite in Cottonwood Canyon. The spring smell of yellow cliffroses fills the air and the frogs are in full voice, with an amazing assortment of sounds, as the first shadows fall over the lovely little waterfall. An iridescent dragonfly and a giant black bee circle over Al's head. A mellow, relaxed evening slips over our little group as we settle down for a spring evening under the stars.

EIGHT H DAY

The lazy atmosphere of a day at camp leaves the four of us in slow motion. No packing up, no boots to put on tired feet, just a chance to lie under the tarp out of the hot sun, dabble fingers in the waterfall, watch the various residents of this ecosystem go about their business, and just enjoy being here. My very favorite bird, the canyon wren, is singing its long, cascading spring song. That music is the essence of the Canyon and I never tire of hearing it.

The day slips by with everyone doing his thing. Interesting how conversation is so minimal between us. Our time clocks are no longer controlled by that other world we left behind. We have all slowed down and are content to just be here, without the complexities of civilization facing us. I loll away the afternoon watching and photographing the frogs. How amazing to see a tiny frog or toad puff itself up to twice its size, fill its pouch and let loose a roar like a burro. It's mating time for sure.

A day at camp allows for soaking lentils for our dinner meal. Carrots are rehydrated and dessert is a strange concoction of carob, honey and almonds, all rolled together. The dishes are washed: two pots, four plates and four spoons. Life is pretty simple here. The candles are lighted and lazy chatter comes and goes as the first star pops into an ebony sky .

NINTH DAY

Awakened by a myriad of bird songs, as a lone frog croaks his way home after a big night on the town. I slowly open my eyes and find that Randy has already left to go birding, but Al is snoozing and Murray is complaining that his sleeping bag smells like garlic. Rock walls are turning coral pink, scorpions are headed home (I hope) and the first fly discovers my nose. My morning yoga is done under a circle of lacy, green cottonwood and redbud trees, with the ever present fragrance of cliffrose bushes filling the air. The birds sing their joyous welcome to the new day. This is my perfect universe where time has stopped!

Our ninth day is our last in the deep canyons. Our campsite tonight will be on Horseshoe Mesa. We fill all our bottles for a dry camp. The days have gone so quickly and a wave of sadness comes over me, knowing that it's all about to end. An easy, but steep hike of only a couple of miles up to the top of the Redwall awaits us. The mesa is a large flat area, totally dry, but covered with an abundance of juniper and piñon trees with wonderful places for camping. An ideal place to end a trip before going out via Grandview Trail, since the views look down and over one of the most beautiful parts of the Canyon. Grandview — the trail is well named.

We pick a spot between the trees as the late afternoon sun leaves a burnished glow over the mesa. Once more I try to come up with an interesting meal for dinner. The food bag is a jumble of odds and ends. A little dried fruit will stew up nicely with leftover almonds. A partly used bag of potato flakes will be our entree, covered with half a package of dried cheese soup, followed by a side of spinach. Ah, a gourmet meal, at least when one is hungry. Not too bad, but I'm beginning to long for a crisp, green salad.

TENTH DAY

Glorious beauty awakens us, with the desert silence wrapping itself over and around the mesa. Sunlit cliffs are peaceful in their solid majesty while we humans hustle to and fro, packing up for the final push up the trail and onto the South Rim. It's time to say our farewells to the Canyon, with its contrasts of burning and land, its bubbling streams and delicate greenery, the noisy, black ravens, the shy, pink rattlers, the blazing sun in its azure sky, the awesome architecture of rock and stone, and the vast height, breadth and depth of this incredible place. All these memories will be filed away as part of the giant jigsaw of the magical Grand Canyon and will give me energy and peace when that other world out there begins to absorb me once again.

CHAPTER 5

Flirting with Winter

Hermit to Grandview • November 1982

October slipped by with too much to do, but the ever-present urge to hike in the Grand Canyon finally surfaced in November as winter was sneaking in on Colorado's high country. Randy, Murray and I quickly decided that we must return before the year ended. The Tonto Trail is our choice, going east from Hermit to Grandview. This is a trip we have wanted to do to fill in a gap on the map of our Canyon meanderings.

FIRST DAY

The weather is sunny but chilly on the South Rim. We leave our car at the trailhead at Grandview and get transportation out to Hermit's Rest. Hermit Creek is our destination today as we hoist up the packs and start the 3,000-foot descent. The Santa Fe Railroad Company built the Hermit Trail in 1910, going from rim to river, as an alternative to the Bright Angel Trail where tourists were charged a dollar.

The trail was named for the hermit Louis Boucher, a French Canadian prospector who lived partway down at Dripping Springs and at his copper mine at Boucher Creek near the river.

The Santa Fe also operated a tourist camp on the ridge near Hermit Creek and took visitors down on mules. An

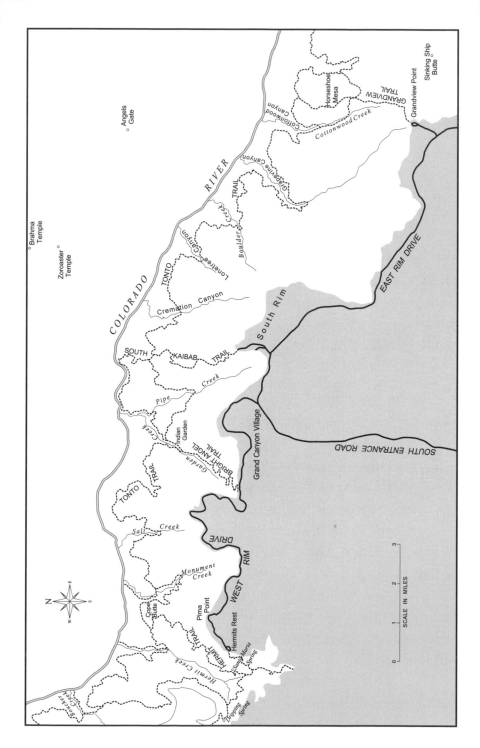

SCALE IN MILES

0   1   2   3

aerial tram lowered supplies the 3,000 feet to the Tonto level from Pima Point.

When the National Park Service took over the Bright Angel Trail, the Hermit route lost its popularity and the camp and the tram were abandoned. The trail, although now unmaintained, is still well established, with neat rock slabs leading down parts of the upper section, and is one recommended for hikers seeking their first wilderness experience before venturing out into the less traveled areas.

The air is cold and we are all wearing long pants instead of the traditional shorts. Reaching Santa Maria Spring, with its old rock shelter, we fill up on water.

Rock slides obscure the trail in the Supai Formation. Narrow, steep, it finally leaves the slide area, where the Supai meets the Redwall, and we descend the switchbacks known as the Cathedral Stairs. This end of the Canyon is almost boxed in, but the views are beautiful to the east through the notch at Cope Butte. Not much greenery except for the piñons and junipers. No cheerful bursts of color from desert flowers to brighten the November somberness. They are resting and storing up energy for their spring debut in this arid land. On through the next long switchbacks on the west slope of Cope Butte. Finally we are on the Tonto with the neatly arranged and leafless blackbrush. Here we step up our pace, finally pass the ranger's cabin on the ridge at the site of the old Hermit Camp and drop down to Hermit Campground.

The November chill settles over our campsite as the sun sets early. Wool hats and mittens go on along with down parkas. Hot soup is welcome as we huddle around the Bluet stove, wishing it were a giant bonfire instead. Several campers are nearby and suddenly there is a great commotion up on a ledge, with people shouting and jumping around. We learn that a spotted skunk has just sprayed their sleeping bags! Now that could be a real disaster. Not much anyone can do to help, and so as darkness quickly descends we light the lanterns and climb into the cozy tents and friendly down bags.

SECOND DAY

A brilliant day, crisp, but warming up fast as we make our way back east along the familiar Tonto, with views down to the slate-colored Colorado River. We are going to Monument Creek on our way to Salt Creek where we'll spend the night. Lots of scrambling over piles of rocks with tall monoliths soaring out of the dry creekbed of Monument. Then out onto the plateau again, with the ubiquitous blackbrush lying in wait for bare legs. Yes, we are back in shorts, enjoying a perfect day. Along the trail are tall, dried century plants, which have had their day of glory and will be toppling over with the next strong winds. Still some green vegetation here and there, mixed with clumps of prickly pear cacti.

Century Plant

We arrive at Salt Creek with its gigantic, dark, flat boulder, ideal for a viewpoint. Our campsite leaves something to be desired, with its cinder-like soil. No place for shorts now as that friendly sun dips quickly behind the rosy cliffs. November definitely has a different feel in the Canyon.

There's a stillness, a somber feeling, no birds sing and only an occasional lizard runs somewhat lethargically over the cool ground. Winter is waiting in the wings and everything reflects that feeling. A spotted skunk passes by, ignoring us.

THIRD DAY

B lue skies again, but a few ominous clouds are scattered along the horizon. It's interesting not knowing the weather forecast—just having to wait and see. No long-range forecasts to worry about. What will be will be, and we'll deal with whatever arrives. Walking the Tonto— what could be better? Long views down to the river are around every bend as we head to Indian Garden, a quite civilized campsite at the junction of the Tonto and the popular Bright Angel Trail. The blue skies are disappearing, but the air is still pleasant as we take the last, long curve leading down to our home for the night.

Indian Garden, the oasis on Garden Creek, has been home to the Indians, the miners, and to thousands of hikers and backpackers under its spreading cottonwoods. These Fremont cottonwood trees were planted in the 1900s and provide welcome shade for travelers going up and down the Bright Angel Trail. But this afternoon we could do without the shade as we set up our tents for a cool evening. Quite a few other campers nearby, and one young man comes over to complain that "something" ate all his gorp. Civilization has corrupted the rodents and they are ready and waiting for supermarket snacks the minute a pack is lowered to the ground. Tonight we eat on a picnic table, which adds a strange dimension to our trip. It somehow seems out of place, but we don't linger over dinner as cold fingers and toes beg for the warmth of down bags.

FOURTH DAY

We leave Indian Garden in morning shadow, drop down and across the Bright Angel Trail, leaving the tourist corridor of the Canyon, and stride out ever eastward over the Tonto Platform towards Cremation Canyon. Sweaters come off as the sun spreads its warm blanket over the plateau, leaving each blackbrush polka-dotting the wide expanse of undulating hills. The views are wider and more expansive here, with a lavender and rose North Rim in the distance. Lunch in Pipe Creek and then out on the rim of the Inner Gorge, where the Kaibab Trail from the South Rim meets the Tonto on its way to the river. Tremendous views down into the gorge where we take the inevitable photos to help temper our long Colorado winters with Canyon slide shows.

The day has been ideal, soaking up all the glories of the Canyon. Now and then an ebony raven circles overhead with a superior glance at the three little figures below, making their way so slowly across the Tonto. That old, mystical feeling accompanies me as my feet take me along the trail—the world outside has been put away and a wave of contentment takes over as I look out at the kaleidoscope of mauves, pinks and reds. The magnitude of this magical place overwhelms me on every trip, always leaving that haunting and compelling urge that keeps me returning year after year.

We are about to cross the Kaibab Trail. We expect to see people, but not what appears! There, right in front of us, are dozens of runners, all properly outfitted in the latest running apparel with their plastic bottles strapped to their waists, some on their way up and some going down. Their faces are twisted into agonizing grimaces as sweat pours off their frightening, red faces. Two have stopped to rest on a boulder and one is vomiting into the bushes, thus expressing his appreciation of the beauty of the Canyon.

Here is my exquisite Grand Canyon and some sort of dreadful ritual is being conducted within its sacred walls! We watch in amazement, wondering if they have any appreciation of where they are. This incredible place has become their outdoor gym, as they race by in their red, white and blue shiny suits. We must get out of here at once and regain our sanity which was so abruptly stripped from us.

We miss the trail and find ourselves up too high, blaming it all on stress caused by the spectacle we have just witnessed. We climb down and finally find the trail to Cremation, our campsite for the night—the name sounds a bit spooky. Supposedly some Indians cremated their dead on the rim and pushed their ashes into the canyon. Caves have been found in the east arm of Cremation, and split twig figurines—little effigies of deer—have been discovered and dated by the carbon-14 method as being from 3,000–4,000 years old. The Tonto was apparently a thoroughfare for those from the early Desert Culture to the Pueblo Anasazi, and finally to the more recent Havasupais and Paiutes.

We find water at the seep spring and a small group of trees by which to camp. A nice evening, slightly overcast and warm. As the noodles bubble merrily, we can't stop talking about the runners on the Kaibab. For sure, this is a National Park and belongs to the public, but there must be rules and regulations that protect the integrity of these special lands which have been set aside. The size of organized groups is limited, hang gliders are no longer allowed in the Canyon and there is at present a loud outcry over the number of planes and helicopters which shatter the silence and often fly below the rim. It's always an ongoing battle to save natural areas from desecration, but it can be done only if those who care are willing to become involved. (Note: Group marathon races are no longer allowed in the Grand Canyon.)

FIFTH DAY

A long trek awaits us today. We will go from Cremation Canyon to Grapevine, over twelve miles. The Tonto Trail is seldom flat and it usually is climbing up or going down a slope. Cairns mark obscure places and drainage crossings. There are numerous animal trails that can often be confusing. Today the trail stays close to the Canyon's edge, with Angel's Gate in the distance, and then enters the sinuosity of Lonetree Canyon where we lunch in threatening weather. Clouds are hanging low, but as the day progresses the sun reappears and off go the jackets as we make our way to Grapevine. Huge clumps of prickly pear cacti appear along the way with a fall-tinged saltbush here and there.

Clouds again as we hike in and out of Boulder Creek. We seem to be doing a lot of dressing and undressing, which means taking off packs each time, not one of my favorite

chores. There's a tech-
nique that Murray
and Randy seem to
do easily and grace-
fully. They lift the
pack onto their knee
and then hoist it up
over one shoulder
and then onto the
next. Always seems
like a good way to
dislocate a shoulder,
so I usually look for a
large boulder where I

Prickly Pear Cactus

can prop it up and work my way, sitting, into it. Packs seem
to have a mind of their own, so one must pamper them.

More changeable weather as the deep, grey clouds sepa-
rate and let shafts of warmth drift over us. We finally reach
Grapevine, where the lone juniper tree awaits our visit. I
miss sleeping under the stars, but it's too chilly and still
looks like rain. When we first backpacked in the Canyon, we
carried only tarps, but after a few blowing, soaking rains, we
resorted to carrying tents, whether needed or not. They add
extra weight to our packs, but they are so nice to have at
times. We still have unpleasant memories of a night at a
Deer Creek campsite, three of us jammed into my daughter's
one-person tent, trying to stay dry, while the wind blew
sideways and a flash flood roared down the creek.

The wind is rustling the few lone leaves on a nearby tree as I open one eye and check out the day. Not too bad. Still those heavy, grey, pompous clouds lurking over the North Rim, but above, the sky is blue. Breakfast, and then into the boots for the long trail out of Grapevine Canyon. An easy day today as we head for Cottonwood. Strolling along the Tonto with stops along the way to stretch out and soak up the sunshine. We munch on dried fruit and almonds and watch the shadows leave their blue silhouettes over the rosy cliffs below Angel's Gate.

Cottonwood looks somber and subdued when we arrive, since the sun has left its deep cleft. A few golden leaves still cling to the trees that give this canyon its name. The little creek flows small and quietly as we look for our favorite campsite by the large, flat boulder. In the distance the last of the sun's rays are painting the canyon walls incredible shades of rose and gold as steel blue clouds, topped with whipped cream billows, hover behind them. Just as we're thinking it can't get any more spectacular, a giant rainbow forms an arch over the Canyon! We stand in awe of the masterpiece before us. Slowly the color fades into the haze, the sun has set, and we shiver as the cold begins to seep into our bones. Dinner is a hurried one as the warmth of our bags invites us into our tents. I fall asleep while a rainbow drifts through my dreams.

The plan was to spend our last night on Horseshoe Mesa, which is our usual tradition, but, with the weather so chilly here in Cottonwood, it could be even colder on the Mesa, so it's decided we'll stay here one more night. The weather alternates between sun and clouds, with showers thrown in for variety. We rig up a tarp between the tents for cooking, cover our packs with plastic bags and hike along Cottonwood Creek. Such a memorable place, even in the fall. Springtime is the magical time, though, with the

Canyon Tree Frog

songs of birds filling the air and the frogs and toads competing for attention. Now it's quiet, except for the wind gusts that suddenly swoop through the nearly bare trees. A few green bushes grow between the large rocks which no longer hold the desert heat. We lunch between showers, bundled in wool ski hats, parkas and gloves.

Afternoon brings a bit of sunshine, but also those same black, threatening clouds, resting behind the sun-splashed vermillion cliffs. Now the wind begins to really blow, the sun is blotted out and rain is falling. We hustle into the tents, zip up the rainflies, and listen to the patter of drops which soon turns into a real downpour. The tent stays dry and snug. Not much to do except curl up in the bag and listen to the noisy serenade overhead. Now and then the deluge lets up, we unzip the doors and greet each other until the next round. Dinner is cooked under the tarp and eaten in our tents. It's going to be a long night with only the wind and rain to entertain us for the next thirteen hours.

EIGHTH DAY

Three disheveled heads peer out of the blue-and-white houses. A soggy, grey day in Cottonwood. As I leave my warm bag and crawl into cool, rather damp clothes, I realize that it is very cold outside. Time to get moving after a warm breakfast. We shake as much moisture off the tents as possible, but they are wet and heavy as we shove them into the bags. We laugh as we hoist up our backpacks, we look like a winter expedition to Mt. Everest instead of a trip to the desert of Arizona. As we leave our campsite the sky clears a bit and there, just above the Redwall, is a suspicious white dusting that gets whiter towards the rim. The first snowstorm of the season has come to the Grand Canyon! I have always wanted to see it in winter. What fun!

The steep trail to Horseshoe Mesa gets the blood circulating. We reach the roofless stone house and unload our packs behind its old, red walls, out of the wind. The sun is valiantly trying to come out as we nibble on snacks. Then out onto the mesa and up the Grandview Trail with its endless views.

Grandview was a popular spot in 1897. Pete Berry, a miner who worked the Last Chance copper mine located in the Redwall on the east side of Horseshoe Mesa, enlarged his cabin on the South Rim and called it the Grand View Hotel. Tourism had come to the Grand Canyon and was more profitable than mining. As we climb up the steep switchbacks, reinforced with cribbing of logs wired to the face of the cliff, we realize that this was the Berry trail leading down to his mine and later used for tourists to visit the mines. When Grand Canyon Village, fifteen miles west, became the railroad stop for the Santa Fe Railroad, Grandview lost its popularity and the trail became a wilderness route, one of the most scenic in the Canyon.

And today it is even more beautiful, with all the high mesas and ledges frosted with white, looking like giant birthday cakes. The higher we climb, the more snow, until we are wading through six inches of the heavy, wet mantle of winter. The sun is out and the Canyon is sparkling clear, fresh and cleansed by the storm. We stop at every viewpoint along the way, experiencing our favorite place in a mood we have not seen before. We look down on the Tonto below us, with the large horseshoe of the mesa just above it, the Sinking Ship and Coronado Butte to the east. In the distance the warm pinks and roses of Brahma Temple and Zoroaster stand regally in the sunlight, followed by other temples, buttes, terraces and mesas blending infinitely into space.

We have filled in another part of the Grand Canyon puzzle and have now hiked, at different times, from South Bass on the west all the way to the eastern Palisades. As we slosh through the snow up to the rim, I feel that same strange nostalgia, sad, but already planning the next trip in the spring. Rim shock is waiting for us as we are thrown abruptly back into that other world.

CHAPTER 6

Old Friends

Grand View, Cottonwood, Grapevine and Horseshoe Mesa

October 1984

FIRST DAY

How great to be back in the Grand Canyon. We leave the crazy tourist scene on the South Rim and head down the Grandview Trail at 10:30 A.M., the perennial heavy packs making the rough, steep trail a challenge as always. Cool and windy on the rim, but then warmer and warmer as we slowly descend. A familiar trail, we must have done it seven times. We look forward to this trip as if renewing our acquaintance with old friends.

Showers are threatening but the sun continues to shine on Horseshoe Mesa where we'll have a lunch stop at the roofless, stone cabin, a relic of futile copper mining. Still some old mine shafts around, a few rusty tin cans, and tailings full of pretty, blue rocks.

Down the break in the Redwall off Horseshoe Mesa, very steep and my toes are complaining as I pick my way down the gravelly trail to Cottonwood Canyon. The wind comes up, with a sprinkling of showers. Randy pops up behind us doing his usual antelope dance down the trail. He claims his "Chinese Shuffle" works well on a very steep, slippery rock pitch. I'm not so sure. It's not working for me.

Water in Cottonwood! Always a happy sight this late in the season. Nobody was sure at the Backcountry Office. Not

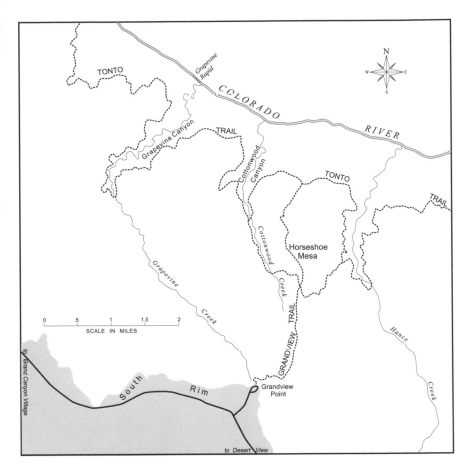

a lot, but enough to get by on. A sudden wind and then
fairly heavy rain. We try to get the tents set up as advertised,
in sixty seconds, and jump in as the next thunder clap
dumps more rain. Nice to be snug and dry as I munch on
dried fruit and the rain beats a steady tune on our little shelter.

In fifteen minutes it's over and the sun is out. Everything is green and glistening. The cottonwoods are getting
their golden fall garb, and they are washed and brilliant. Angel's Gate is in the distance with dark, storm clouds behind
it, setting off its pink majesty. Murray is seventy and I'm

sixty-four and we can still make it down into the Canyon, heavy pack and all, maybe not in the manner of antelopes, but carefully and steadily.

Tarantula

It's a special place here. A rattler crosses our path and a fuzzy tarantula ambles over a rock. The canyon wren is only chirping, not its lovely spring cadence, but she's here and that in itself, along with the squawking ravens make it seem like coming home after a year-and-a-half away.

SECOND DAY

A partly sunny and fresh morning after a heavy downpour during the night. We awake to the sound of rolling rocks and a thundering roar at 7:00 A.M. Quiet, almost empty, little Cottonwood Creek has turned into a foaming, red flash flood! We scramble down to the falls and watch the red water pour over the grey slickrock, forming large piles of foamy bubbles as the water races down to the Colorado River far below.

We head west for Grapevine Canyon. Looks like the skies are clearing and that old familiar desert heat appears as we walk the undulating Tonto Plateau, with the blackbrush clawing at bare legs. The views are wide, long and breathtaking, from the Palisades on the east to Angel's Gate across the river, with tremendous drop-offs and tantalizing glances down to the brown Colorado. We can hear the sound of Grapevine Rapid. It looks exciting, even from here, as we remember its large hole just waiting to swallow rafts.

Longer than I remember to Grapevine. Nice little oasis stop at a spring along the way cools hot toes in its running water. Then more walking. The hills and cliffs are dark and mysterious ahead of us, lost in the haze, looking like the mystical mountains of Tibet. Somewhere in that misty distance is our camp for the night. At last we descend to the lone juniper tree where we camped in November 1982 in a cold rainstorm while the wind roared, making cooking dinner a miserable affair.

Tonight it's a different story. Warm and windless as the stars make their appearance. It's dark at 7:00 P.M. so it's early to bed these October nights. The dinner pans are being investigated by evening visitors. Randy puts rocks on each upside down pan and things quiet down. A large owl flies over to a nearby cliff hunting his evening meal, and a bat makes a sharp right turn as it snags an unlucky insect. A slight silver glow comes from the east as a late moon makes its way over the black cliffs—and so to sleep.

THIRD DAY

A day at camp in Grapevine Canyon. Murray and I try going downstream, but a large drop-off discourages us, so we head upstream, bushwhacking through the willows, then into a lovely, narrow canyon of deep pools and slickrock walls. We wade through one, only to be stopped by walls too slick and steep to negotiate. So downstream again and back up a manageable route to a string of small pools gurgling their happy way downcanyon. And here I sit, naked and content, about as far away from civilization as one can get, surrounded by rugged, pink canyon walls, a vivid ultramarine sky overhead. An ominous, large, orange wasp checks out leftover summer blossoms and a blue-violet dragonfly with lacy, iridescent wings skims over the water. Murray sneezes his usual resounding three sneezes, and I worry about rock slides! High above on an almost black rock grow delicate green bushes with tiny, yellow flowers, nature's wonderful contrast of hardness and softness.

Back to camp for a shampoo in a cooking pot. Clean hair is a luxury after a few days of dirt and sweat. As the sun quickly dries my hair, Randy appears. He made it downstream for several miles, but no way was found on down to the river without a rope.

I investigate the soaking lentils and discover there are enough to feed at least six! A good meal for those layover days at camp. Night descends at 6:30 P.M. as we light the little candle lanterns. A black beetle stands on his head when I touch his rear end. The night creatures stir as the crickets sing their various songs. A cloudbank builds in the northeast. Can our beautiful weather be changing? The Milky Way gets a soft haze over it as we slip into our down bags.

FOURTH DAY

At 6:30 A.M. a suspicious wind comes and goes, and soft, see-through clouds drift above as I lie in the tent with my head out. Back to Cottonwood today over the Tonto Plateau. A favorite place to be unless the temperatures soar. As I look out over this dry, prickly landscape, surrounded by towering buttes and monoliths, how comfortable and familiar it seems. We have seen no one for two days. It is so satisfying to know there are still places in this crowded, frantic world where one can forget everything and simply watch a weed waving in the breeze, or wonder at the strange shape of a prickly pear cactus.

We pack up and leave Grapevine Canyon under a light overcast, with a gentle wind blowing across the Tonto. Deep, purple clouds hang over the North Rim, intensifying the pink of Vishnu's Temple in the distance. Sun breaks through for a dried pineapple break. Deep, jagged views to the river appear as we make our way around the sinuous trail leading to Cottonwood. Lunch in a terraced canyon, where deer tracks lead to a small pool of water. Sweaters come off as the sky becomes striped with bands of blue breaking the cloud cover. On the trail again, when Randy stops suddenly as he spots a greenback lesser goldfinch — what a beauty — brilliant, yellow-green breast with a black-and-white tail and a distinctive song that gave his presence away.

FIFTH DAY

After a star-filled night and a bright, late moon, we again awaken to a little wind rustling the cottonwood leaves. Pink and white puffs of clouds go floating by. Another storm system? Today we are headed up to Horseshoe Mesa and there the wind does blow. But now it's only 7:00 A.M. and I'm still warm and cozy in my bag. A few chirps and tweets from the birds, but the night-singing crickets have gone to sleep and it's very quiet between wind gusts. The desert can be so silent, silence that is hard to find anywhere else. It seems to fill every crack and crevice, cover the buttes and mesas, and slide into the canyons. It envelops you and fills you with peace and contentment like nothing else I've ever known.

We head for Horseshoe Mesa, up a new trail for us, out east onto the Tonto and then up the west arm of the mesa. Steep but pleasant. A cold wind on top greets us as we dig into our packs for jackets, long pants, hats and mittens. A little gain in elevation changes seasons quickly. A large juniper tree offers some wind protection as we huddle over a quick lunch. The mesa is a favorite spot with the three of us. Its views are incredible and, though it's only three miles from the rim, it is so large that seldom does one meet others.

A storm is brewing in the north. Great, grey clouds of rain and snow slip between the towers and pinnacles, far across the river. Looks like winter over there on the North Rim which is 1,000 feet higher than the South Rim. As the wind continues to buffet us it's beginning to feel like winter right here.

We walk out to a high point looking down into Cottonwood and east to Desert View, with even a glimpse of Hance Rapid foaming away upriver. Wotan's Throne and Vishnu Temple are catching the rays of an elusive sun as we hunch down in front of large rocks to avoid the persistent wind. The sturdy juniper trees hug the land as violent blasts race through their foliage. We watch the storm cover the North Rim and, suddenly, the wind on our mesa dies down and the sun appears, warm and delightful. Bodies relax, heavy jackets come off as we stroll along the edge. With our binoculars we spot a group of campers far below, headed for Cottonwood. We watch their tiny forms puttering around their campsite from our vantage point 1,200 feet above.

The mesa is covered with dead agave, the "century" plants that take twenty to twenty-five years to bloom and reach heights of over ten feet and then, having had their day of glory, topple and die, looking eventually like old mops left by untidy maids.

The storm continues to roll across the North Rim, the desert pink of the distant cliffs dulled by grey, misty sweeps of rain and snow. Our sunny respite is over as the wind brings sleet and cold, so we rush back to the security of our little blue-and-white houses.

Dinner is eaten inside as we pass our pots from tent to tent. The wind blows stronger as the nylon rainflies flap incessantly. Too much wind and cold to even think of rinsing out the pots and pans. We toss them out of the tents and settle in for a long, noisy night of wind and rain.

Just as I'm dozing off, I hear Randy's tent zipper open and a four-letter word flies out the opening. The spotted skunks have discovered the pots

Spotted Skunk

and pans and Randy's tent! On go the flashlights, as those really lovely little creatures scurry out of the light, their white, feathery tails waving in the wind. Randy hangs the pans high up on the branches of a nearby juniper and we settle down once more. Someone says, "Do skunks climb trees?" No answer, as we sink into slumber once more. Again we are rudely awakened to the rattles and bangs of those annoying dirty pots. Yes, skunks do climb trees. We give up, the skunks win and, as I slip down into my bag, I'm just grateful that we didn't all get sprayed.

SIXTH DAY

Sunrise on Horseshoe Mesa. It's twenty-nine degrees as I sit on an outcropping of rock looking down into a dark and mysterious Grand Canyon. I'm encased in my bag looking like a large, red caterpillar, waiting for the sun to work its way over the distant cliffs, a ritual not to be missed if one is lucky enough to camp high on a Canyon mesa. Slowly the highest towers and buttes turn rosy pink, as long, cascading shadows spill over the lower cliffs. The Coconino Sandstone on the South Rim turns sunny and bright, highlighting the multitudes of junipers which cling to its rocky sides.

The sun is up for sure and I relax my frigid posture as its rays begin to penetrate my down bag. The bottom of the Canyon is still in cold shadow, but up here a few birds are glorifying in the warmth as the silence is broken by their fall sounds and chatter. Sunshine is everywhere, the fat junipers are soaking up its rays, looking green and satisfied. Deep, purple shadows accentuate the distant cliffs as the sun slowly works its way into the last deep clefts and gorges. And now the sun is officially up and in charge throughout the Grand Canyon.

Breakfast, and then the reality that we are headed up and out. The Grandview Trail is so satisfying, its switchbacks going back and forth with spectacular panoramic views at each turn. I find I'm stopping more and more often as the end of the trip comes closer. I look for excuses to take photos or just look back, anything to prolong my stay.

But now I'm on the rim and must face civilization. It hasn't changed—the buses, the tourists taking their quick looks and then back to their cars. But I walk through the crowds feeling quite special to have spent those six short days below the rim, satisfied for the moment—until that haunting longing begins again and I must return once more to the Grand Canyon.

CHAPTER 7

New Horizons

Boucher to South Bass • April 1985

FIRST DAY

It's spring and the Canyon calls. So here we are, starting on another jaunt, eleven days, from Hermit's Rest and the Boucher Trail westward to South Bass. We tried to do it two years ago but the weather caused it to be called off, primarily because of the thirty-mile dirt, rutted road to where one must leave a car at the South Bass Trailhead in order to get back to civilization. Rain can make the last part of this road totally impassable, but today one VW bus is safely at the trailhead and we are on our way.

Down the Hermit Trail. The cool, windy morning becomes warmer as we leave the higher Coconino Sandstone and arrive at the turnoff to Dripping Springs. We have carried very little water down, so now it's up the half-mile to the spring with a daypack full of empty canteens. A lovely little oasis, under a large rock overhang, where one small strand of crystal water drops fifty or so feet from the spring above. A slow process, filling six bottles, while the wind sends that single stream of water back and forth, missing the openings most of the time. No hurry, though, in this pleasant spot, with a canyon wren keeping me company with her spring song.

I load my daypack with the now heavy plastic canteens and join Murray, who is guarding the packs from curious

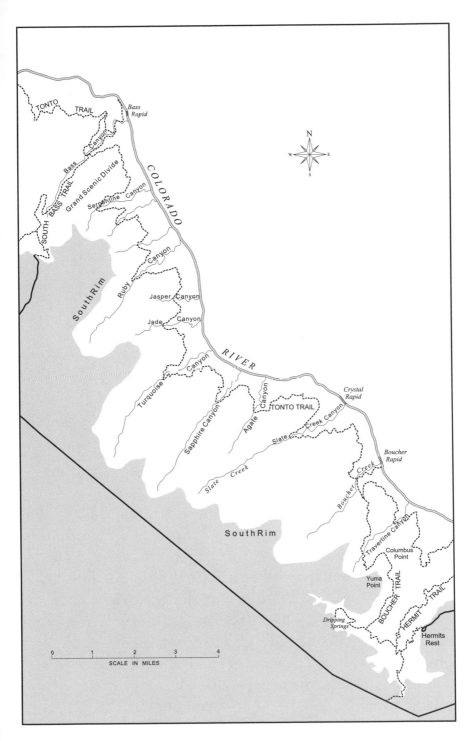

TONTO TRAIL
Bass Rapid
Bass Canyon
SOUTH BASS TRAIL
Grand Scenic Divide
Serpentine Canyon
COLORADO
South Rim
Ruby Canyon
Jasper Canyon
Jade Canyon
RIVER
Turquoise Canyon
Sapphire Canyon
Agate Canyon
TONTO TRAIL
Crystal Rapid
Slate Creek Canyon
Slate Creek
Boucher Rapid
Boucher Creek
Travertine Canyon
Columbus Point
South Rim
Yuma Point
BOUCHER TRAIL
HERMIT TRAIL
Dripping Springs
Hermits Rest

N
W E
S

0   1   2   3   4
SCALE IN MILES

and hungry rodents. Randy has caught up and we lunch together on the dark red ground amidst clusters of white phlox and purple pea plants. Springtime green illuminates the land. Gnatcatchers dart in and out of the Mormon tea bushes and grey-green sage.

Murray and I reluctantly fill our packs with eight new pounds of water-weight each. Suddenly they are miserable to carry, pulling on the shoulders and pushing on the hips. A dry camp tonight, so we have little choice, although Randy, who hiked down three days ago, saw potholes along the trail and is counting on those. If they are dry, he will have a long trip back to Dripping Springs.

A splendid walk with views to the river. The word view is totally inadequate. It's such an unreal sight to look anywhere in the Grand Canyon. There's so much to grasp. Even seeing it as often as we have, it still overwhelms and I often wonder why I keep trying to describe it. Someone asked me why do we go so often to the Canyon, haven't we seen everything? How does one answer that? One doesn't. When you love something you want more of it. Do you ever tire of seeing a sunset or hearing a meadowlark on a fresh spring morning?

We camp the first night just off the Boucher Trail. Randy has found his potholes and is feeling smug as we unload our six heavy bottles of water. We are on a promontory, with Yuma Point looming above us and Columbus Point below, and can see from the Palisades, east of Desert View, to the Powell Plateau and the Muav Saddle to the west. The green pea soup of the Colorado River and the white of Granite Rapid are below us. The wind is gusty and it's cold on this exposed rim. Up go the houses, well secured with tiedowns to large rocks. Cups of hot soup warm our innards. A young moon is overhead and a few stars are peeking out among the scattered clouds. So good to be back under the Canyon's canopy.

SECOND DAY

The thermometer registers thirty-eight degrees, but the weak sun feels good and the wind has spent itself. Piñon jays, the color of juniper berries, flock to Randy's potholes for their morning drink. Annoying tourist sightseeing planes drone overhead and their shattering echoes upset the solitude and invade our privacy. We break camp and hike along the Supai until we reach the very steep and challenging break leading down Travertine Canyon. Not one of my favorite descents, but the white, blooming Fendler bushes, the serviceberry blossoms and the yellow cliffroses, with their overwhelming sweet smells, keep my mind off what's ahead. The very beginning of the Travertine trail is so steep, one must go down backwards, careful not to get the pack caught on the protruding rocks. Then it's just a matter of negotiating the extremely steep route, with handholds provided by those same obliging bushes we used last time. Not so bad this trip, but the old knees complain a bit.

Lunch under a rock overhang out of the wind. Snow showers are filling up the Canyon over on the north side. Definitely below-normal temperatures this time of year. We cross the "Boy Scout Burn," which was caused by a bonfire lighted as a signal for help and which promptly got out of control. Bet the Scouts hate that legacy. The Redwall is next, always steep and rocky.

This whole trail is considered one of the steepest off the South Rim. Watching one's feet and checking out each rock, to keep from plummeting into space, consumes us. We stop along the way to relieve our aching knees and screaming toes and are soothed by the spring display of orange globe mallow, blue larkspur, cream waxy yucca blossoms and magenta hedgehog cactus flowers.

Boucher Camp at last. Hard to believe that Boucher came down that trail often in the twenty years he lived here, looking for valuable ore and hauling it out on his white mule, a match to his flowing white hair. He grew an orchard and his solitude was only occasionally broken by a visit from a riverman. Remnants of his stone house and an old mine shaft still remain.

The weather is threatening and the expected desert warmth of the deep Canyon is missing. We have the place to ourselves, except for a pleasant couple from Nebraska, who are staying over a day to heal blisters. This is their first visit to the Canyon and they will be going out tomorrow up the Hermit Trail. She is a weaver and he a solar engineer.

Dinnertime and the menu lists kale, Ramen noodles concocted with eggplant, zucchini and tomato soup. Quite tasty. Dried fruit for dessert and we are full and happy. The moon tries to show its young face, but the clouds are rolling in and we just make it to our tents as the first drops of rain begin. As the rain increases it becomes a soothing go-to-sleep sound after a long day of hiking.

THIRD DAY

No hurry today. We'll just enjoy Boucher Creek under a sky which has turned blue and promising. Large yuccas are in bloom, with lily-like flowers still heavy with last night's raindrops. I stroll over to the roofless stone house that Boucher lived in for so many years. It is filled with ancient, rusty cans and a broken iron bucket. I try to imagine the life he led as a hermit in the depths of the mighty Grand Canyon.

This afternoon we all walk down to the Colorado River, through a beautiful little canyon and out to the white, sandy beach. The river is flowing fast, as usual, and Boucher Rapid is giving its customary roar. A large sand dune has formed above the beach, a perfect place to stretch out in the sun. The river glides past, and across the wide highway of water is the black Vishnu Schist of this Inner Gorge. As the river flowed west across the rising Kaibab Plateau, it cut into the older rocks until it exposed the ancient, twisted, tortured and metamorphosed roots of forgotten mountains that towered as high as the Himalayas, imprisoning the river in the somber recesses of the Inner Gorge. Murray spots a flash of stark white, which becomes a large snowy egret. An exciting sight against the two-billion-year-old schist as it preens its immaculate white feathers and balances on its long, spindly legs and yellow feet.

A trip to the Canyon is always more complete after a visit to the river, that tremendous force which is still carving its way through the rock walls. And, even though it is controlled by the hand of man now, its power continues, with the dozens of side canyons often sending torrents of water into its flow. Hard to believe that it starts as a tiny, alpine stream near Granby, Colorado.

We leave the noise of the river and rapids and are quickly into the silence of Boucher Creek as the late sun leaves its Midas touch on quiet pools filled with young tadpoles.

Swift

Food bags are taken down from their hanging branches and dinner is prepared, as a half-moon and upside-down Big Dipper look down upon this tiny group. The poorwills are calling, but the most welcome sound of all is the frogs. We had all eagerly looked forward to their evening music, but nary a sound last night, just too cold for them to venture out of the mud, but tonight there's a mini-symphony which tells us it's spring for sure. The swifts and swallows are bug-darting in the evening sky. Our candle lanterns are lighted and night begins.

FOURTH DAY

Today we leave Boucher and head west for Slate Creek. I start out first and wait on the Tonto, sitting in a garden of yellow brittlebush. It's warm and cloudy. White clouds are tucked in among the distant canyons. Everything has a hushed and subdued feeling. Birds are singing quietly, a soft breeze rustles the sparse vegetation and cools my wet back. The somber blackbrush is now a gentle green, and dotted among them are the vivid, vibrant blooms of prickly pear cacti. Delicate petals of hot pink, soft rose, and coral grow casually between dangerous spines. Now and then a single branch of intense blue or purple larkspur pops up among the white daisies which compete with yellow brittlebush flowers. A tall, creamy-flowered yucca towers over a tiny, wild onion plant, almost missed in the colorful display.

A twisting trail today with many weather changes. Lunch is on a viewpoint above the red Colorado River. The rains in the side canyons have washed down and have given it its true name, "color red." No signs of others, just the way we like the Tonto—empty, vast and open. Left our packs on the trail and walked over to the edge of the Canyon to glimpse Crystal Rapid, a #10 on river ratings, an exciting white water maneuver in a river raft. Finally into Slate Creek where we've camped before under a lone juniper tree in a lovely open canyon with water running over the slickrock terraces. As I pour the cool water out of a pan over my hot and sticky body, a shower passes over and I'm instantly rinsed off.

The vegetarian chili simmers and the three of us settle in for the evening. The sky darkens after the shower, followed by a magical rainbow arching across an ashen sky. Too early for the frogs to tune up, but a gnatcatcher sings his sleazy, little song as a mockingbird expertly imitates a rock wren. And in the distance is the haunting melody of the canyon wren.

Tomorrow we head for canyons, trails and campsites unknown to us, a week of walking through canyons named after jewels, before we reach Bass Canyon and hike the eight miles up to Randy's bus at the trailhead.

The names string out along the Tonto like a necklace of precious stones—Agate, Sapphire, Turquoise, Jasper, Jade, Ruby, Quartz, Emerald. Very inspiring! We are reminded that the guidebooks are correct when they state: "Route find-ing ability is a necessity." The Tonto, for many miles west-ward, is more of a route than a trail and, if we don't find water at our planned campsites, we will have to continue on in the heat to another side canyon. The alternative is to find a feasible route down to the river, which would be difficult at best. The Backcountry Office has had no information on this area for several weeks.

As the days go by, it becomes more difficult and less im-portant to keep track of time. Life becomes sleeping, eating, walking, looking and experiencing the Canyon moods. Rain again tonight, and then the moon. It's never the same in that big sky overhead.

FIFTH DAY

We are up at 5:00 A.M. to a chorus of bird songs. The wrens, the mockingbird, the black-throated spar-row all send their music through Slate Creek Can-yon, as the day sparkles after last night's rain. Seven miles to Sapphire over the Tonto. New land and new views. Off we go!

The desert heat is out in full force today, but a good breeze makes it tolerable. The trail is very vague and we lose it completely going into Agate Canyon. The few cairns must have been knocked over or never existed. We thrash around through prickly bushes until we find a way through a gully and finally into Agate. A large boulder provides welcome shade for our lunch stop. No water here, just hot and baked by the sun. Everyone is a little subdued, wondering about water in Sapphire which will be home for tonight, if there is water. Two-and-a-half miles to go and we'll know, but as we look down into this side canyon, it looks discouragingly dry. If there is no water in Sapphire we have to hike three more miles to Turquoise.

The sun is scorching and we are experiencing the true desert environment, thirst that our limited tepid water can't quench and a nagging worry about water ahead. As we hike along, each with his own thoughts, Randy stops abruptly, and there, right in front of him is a beautiful bighorn sheep, a ram, with large, full curled horns! We stand staring at each other. No one moves while he contentedly chews his cud. Murray comes along just in time to see him slowly saunter up the hill where he continues to stand and observe us.

Bighorn Sheep

What a truly wild sight. It made our day and, to make the day even better, we find lots of clear water cascading down the slickrock of Sapphire.

We rinse off with the precious water, put on our sneakers and find a ledge out of the sun, stretch out, feeling most content. A blue-grey gnatcatcher becomes annoyed as Murray mimics her call. I watch a large bee search for sweets. All thoughts leave my mind. I'm just under a ledge in Sapphire Canyon in the Grand Canyon of Arizona.

Around 5:00 P.M. the air begins to cool a bit. No need for tents tonight. A half-moon lights the sky, the frogs begin to sing and an acrobatic display by the resident bats provides the evening's entertainment.

SIXTH DAY

Only a short hike to Turquoise Canyon today—just three miles. Murray and I leave Randy at the campsite to catch up with us later. Since we are slower, this method works well. It feels especially good to be walking this morning and I strike out ahead, following the cairns which are spaced quite far apart. After walking a while I look back and there is no Murray. I wait on a hill. I wait and wait. He was right behind me, where could he be? I leave my pack on the hill, where it's easy to spot, and start walking back for nearly a mile. Still no Murray. I finally meet Randy who also hasn't seen him. I go back up the hill while Randy checks a small side gully.

As I stand on the hill, seeing no one, an odd feeling comes over me. This is a vast, hostile land, with no way out for probably another twenty miles. One could get frantic. Everything is so big and I feel so small as I look through my binoculars in all directions for a human form. I call, I blow on my whistle. Silence, frightening silence all around me.

It seems forever before I hear Randy call, way in the distance. I put on my pack and walk in the direction of his voice. He's found Murray's tracks! We follow them and there stands Murray, worrying about us! Seems there were two sets of cairns. I followed the scenic route overlooking the river and Murray followed the inland route, since I was already out of his sight. So much for the adrenaline rush of the day.

We detour for a spectacular view of the river, and then back into the sinuosity called Turquoise Canyon. It looks dry and unpromising, but we spot a little wet sand and follow it to a merry seep. Once again we seek out a shady ledge, avoiding the sun as we spread our peanut butter on crackers for an early lunch. Not a lot of camping choices. The only one is in full sun, so it's under the ledge until the canyon wall finally eliminates that solar blast furnace.

The hours slip by. The feel of this trip is one of complete wildness. We have seen no one, trails are hardly visible and few people come this way. In summer the water dries up in each of these canyons, so springtime is the only reasonable time to do this trip. Two golden eagles lazily drift around a high pinnacle and an incredible yellow-and-black butterfly drinks from the seep. I use our new high-tech water purifier to slowly fill the canteens from the tiny strand of water that comes out of the side of the dry streambed. Probably no need to purify this water, but I have time on my hands and it's a pleasant, almost meditative process to push the small pump in and out, in and out...

A lazy day and, as evening descends and welcome shade covers the campsite, I sit on a rock and look at this strange land. To be sure, it's hostile, prickly, often uninviting, almost waterless, no one within miles. I'm encircled by high, red walls, a tiny speck in this mammoth place. Why am I here? It's an intrigue with the Grand Canyon, a challenge, longing for wild, unspoiled places. To spend eleven days, dependent on my physical body, the food and essentials in my pack, the water sources always five to seven miles apart, not really knowing what each day will bring — it's all there and we three have the mental ability to enjoy it all, good parts and bad. It's where I want to be.

As I wash from a pan, sitting naked in the dry rocky streambed, letting the cool water from our faithful seep pour over me, I feel a closeness to Mother Earth. Easy to feel my roots in this earth without man-made wars to encase me,

Scott's Oriole

radios to inform me, or stereos to soothe me. Strange to think that civilization is out there, doing its frantic thing as I listen to the song of a brilliant yellow-and-black Scott's Oriole. Randy has washed his clothes, leaving them on a prickly bush to dry — no clothespins needed here — and with his binoculars around his neck, clad only in his boots and birthday suit, he takes off to look for a peregrine falcon he thinks he saw earlier.

But I'm content to just sit and let the rhythm of the desert be my time clock. How peaceful it is. How easy to forget the heavy pack on one's back, the aching feet, the beating pulse in a hot head, the sore shoulders and muscles and the knowledge that if there's really a serious problem one might not make it out of here. It's all part of what we are doing and enjoying, and I wouldn't trade places with anyone as I sit contentedly on a hard, warm boulder in Turquoise Canyon this evening in May.

SEVENTH DAY

L eft Turquoise very early, before the hot sun hit our camp. It'll be a scorcher today. Not a cloud. On goes the wet hat before I've gone a mile. Once again over the Tonto, through the familiar blackbrush, amidst the sudden surprises of magenta cactus blooms and delicate mariposa lilies, growing in gravelly, impossible soil. Great long view of the river, stops for the ERG drink, the lemonade that tastes awful but replenishes minerals and salts lost by the heat and exercise. It seems to help. Big, long and dry sinuosities are ahead today. Oh, to be a raven and be able to soar over these deep abysses instead of having to plod our way in and out again and again. The names, Jade and Jasper, are lovely but the canyons are dry and stifling hot since we lose the Tonto breeze in each one. Six miles to Ruby. Doesn't sound too far.

We can make good time on the Tonto Plateau, but the pace is slow in and out of the side canyons. We turn towards Ruby around noon. The heat is intense. Back, back into the canyon over the boulder-strewn trail. A welcome rock shelf provides shade as we three limp hikers drink our warm water, wet our hats and scarves, and then wearily hoist our houses onto our backs once again as we search for our next campsite in Ruby. It's stifling hot as we descend into our

Mariposa Lily

destination. The only flat camping site is treeless, so we rig a tarp over a ten-foot-high boulder and tie the ends to bushes. It helps a bit, but the temperature stays at 102 degrees so we unenthusiastically fix lunch. Interesting to recall that it was 38 degrees just three days ago up on the Supai.

There must be a better place in this canyon to spend the afternoon. I walk down the cascading slickrock with its delicate flow of water and find a ledge in the shade beside a pool deep enough to sit in. I try not to disturb the tadpoles or the spider web across it, as I sit in absolute ecstasy, feeling my hot skin cool down. Then back under the shady ledge and to my small, rather dull paperback book. The soothing sound of running water makes it difficult to keep my eyes on the words. Randy and Murray join me as thunderheads pile up on the rim. How welcome a shower would be, but just as the rain looks about to open up, our resident blast furnace evaporates everything into the blue void above. And there is only wind.

We are happy to see the sun go behind a wall at 4:15 P.M. and, like the birds who have been silent during the heat, we now become active as we go about our chores. Murray is purifying the water and curious Randy is exploring up the canyon. I rummage in the food bags, looking for an interesting meal, as the first frog heralds the evening. The night creatures are getting ready, as the temperature becomes comfortable. This is really a lovely canyon, lush and junglelike. The cliffrose bushes still have a few fragrant blossoms, the squaw plant flowers are gone, but some tall century plants are nearly ready to burst into giant, blooming hummingbird feeders. The mesquite trees look dead, but looking closely, one can see tiny green leaves. Each growing thing has its own timetable in the desert.

EIGHTH DAY

Up early at 4:45 A.M. as the last stars begin to fade in the lightening sky. Cool enough for sweaters, as we quickly pack up to beat the heat of midday hiking. The morning sun comes over the first rim in the distance as we are having breakfast on the Tonto. Only five miles to cover today, with our goal Serpentine Canyon another unknown—terrain-wise and water-wise. Leaving so early we can have time to spend in each canyon, time to be lazy, search for new flowers or watch a beetle who has come to visit. We arrive at Serpentine at 10:30 A.M. and, since it's too far to go to Bass in the heat of the day, we'll stay here. Not the most attractive of canyons, very narrow with only a small amount of water. There is little to explore here, so keeping cool as possible, dozing a bit in the shadow of a boulder, fills our day.

But a new ingredient today. People! Two young fellows on their way to Ruby and eventually Hermit, stop for water. They are firefighters from the South Rim who have a few days off for a backpack. Murray and I find it a bit strange to be social after six days of seeing no one but each other. Randy simply lies under the boulder and is silent, refusing to break the spell of the Canyon. On their way they go and life settles down again to just being here.

Thankfully the sun has set at 4:00 P.M. in our narrow world of rock, and Murray and I come to life. The food bag is getting lighter and the evening meal becomes more of a challenge as supplies dwindle. I sit on my usual evening boulder, a very hot boulder, still full of solar power, and sort out little plastic bags of dehydrated food. The mourning doves land in the streambed, looking for water. A canyon wren sings her happy cadence somewhere high on the Redwall above, while a green lizard scurries over the hot rocks. A little boxed-in canyon. I'd rate it in the Motel 6 category as far as amenities, but it has water, which brings it up to at least a Hilton. But when night comes and that almost full moon appears and I lie under its silvery glow in my sleeping bag—there's no place that can compare.

NINTH DAY

A hot day ahead, so up at 5:00 A.M., fumbling in the dark trying to pack my stuff in the backpack. Belongings should be getting smaller but instead they seem to be getting bigger. I wet my hat and scarf, my desert air conditioners, in the tiny pools of water, when suddenly I am joined by bats who are gracefully skimming the water for morning drinks. They come by so close, Randy and I can almost feel their wings, but their radar is in perfect control so that they never quite touch us. What amazing, silent, flying mammals. A splendid way to start the day.

A long way out of Serpentine Canyon, two miles before

breakfast at our favorite restaurant on the Tonto. Today the special is a cheese omelet served beside the blackbrush with scattered clouds shading the early rising sun and views which never fail to astonish. In the distance the Holy Grail Butte looks like an upside-down funnel. High above is our final destination at Bass Trailhead, 4,400 vertical feet from the river, where we are now headed. But before we can get there we must cross the Scenic Divide, a gigantic ridge which separates the east canyon from the west. Then up a short way into Bass Canyon and down again two and a half miles to the river where we'll spend tonight.

So back to the trail, such as it is, one foot after another. Very muggy today, and hot when the sun skirts a cloud and beams its full intensity on three minute hikers. Randy, with his eagle eyes, spots a desert black-throated sparrow's nest with two tiny, recently-hatched babies and an egg ready to pop. The nest is beautifully formed and tucked into a very sharp and prickly blackbrush, secure and comfortable.

Down Bass Canyon—very hot. We find a big pothole and purify water for the trip to the river. We dislike the idea of drinking the Colorado River water. The silt has to settle and, even after purifying it, you think of all the stuff that gets dumped in Lake Powell, the Little Colorado River and all the hundreds of side canyons.

And so down to the river, a tough drop-off at the end, over hot black rocks that one can barely touch, as we creep down the steep descent to the beach. Now the red river, the white sand, the heat bouncing back over our hot bodies. My wet hat is no longer even damp, my head is pounding from the heat as we struggle through the scorching sand to a little rocky cover with tamarisk trees. Nice surprise to find small potholes of clear water at our feet. No river water for us!

We wash our grimy shirts and shorts in the river and they come out looking just as dirty, but with a little less aroma. Afternoon is spent on the sand when it's cloudy and under the rocks when it's sunny. It thunders and even showers as we watch a group of wooden dories go by. A couple of kayakers wave before getting swallowed up in Bass Rapid. Another group appears on the water and I drool as I watch the boatman guzzle cold beer. Suddenly, someone yells, "Dottie and Murray!" They row off to the side quickly before entering the rapid and it's Karen and Doug from Aspen. What a small world. We are offered cold beer, the first cold thing we've had since we were at Columbus Point, nine days ago. A treat, for sure. They visit for a while and then hop into their raft and veer out into the river for their encounter with the rapids.

Once again it's just the three of us, watching, listening, the river going by, the growling of the rapids, the sand, the breeze, the minutes slowly slipping away. A little jolt from the outside world. Now only a memory.

As I photograph the rapids at sunset, three hikers arrive down the black rocks. Strange how territorial one becomes. I resent their arrival, an intrusion on our private beach! But I remind myself that this beach is owned by the United States public so I force myself to exchange pleasantries and even tell them where the fresh water is located. Three nice, young folks, graduates of the University o Arizona, back for a Canyon reunion.

Our initial plan was to spend all day, and tomorrow, at the river and then hike out in the late afternoon and dry camp three or four miles up. However, we decide one day here is enough. Funny how we all admit we like the high country better. The river and the beach are pleasant only for a short period of time and then we three mountain people want to get out and up. So in the morning we will do just that—bright and early.

One needs to get to the river at the beginning or end of a trip just for that sense of completion, since the Colorado River is such an integral part of the Canyon experience. It is the reason for the Canyon. Even though dams and too many boaters have changed the face of the river, it is still a mighty force. Boating permits are limited, but it seems like there are still too many issued, diluting the wilderness experience that used to exist. But, different strokes for different folks, I keep telling myself.

Night on the beach is special, even for mountain people. As I spread the tarp and my bag on the soft, warm sand, I stretch out in satisfaction and watch an almost full moon poke its silvery face over the high walls of the Canyon. The river's music ripples over the sand as the rapids' lullaby sends me quickly into dreamland.

TENTH DAY

In the grey light of early morning we shake the sand out of our belongings, as a snowy egret watches for fish on a nearby rock. We climb up the black rocks, which are only warm now, and head for the potholes for breakfast. Water is purified for all our bottles. It's a long trip and dry camp ahead. The packs which had become lighter are suddenly miserable again as we leave for the 3,000-foot climb to the Esplanade, our destination for tonight.

The Redwall is surprisingly short, but instead we are faced with a long and steep Supai. Quite a change from the dry Tonto. As the elevation increases, so does the vegetation.

The piñon and juniper trees are thicker as we near the Esplanade and the air is cooler and fresher. At an excellent viewpoint we stop for lunch, looking down into Bass Canyon. It seems so far away now, just as the South Rim did yesterday. Two rangers and then a group of backpackers going down the trail pass us. Civilization is creeping into our wilderness experience.

Glad to reach the level Esplanade with our water-laden packs. It is very beautiful. We have left summer below us and are back into spring. Moving feet can perform miracles. The Fendler bush and the cliffrose are in full bloom and the air is filled with their perfume. We find a perfect camping spot, with large piñon pines and a spectacular view looking down into Bass Canyon. Found out later that this same spot was where Bass had his tourist camp years ago. Good choice.

Our tenth and last night. We leave in the morning for the final three-mile hike to Randy's car at the South Bass Trailhead. Another memorable experience, a real wilderness one for the most part. We have had every kind of weather, with a good portion of moonlight thrown in at night. Our food is almost gone, we're tan, scratched and very dirty. A comb can hardly make its way through my grimy hair. As I sit on the red rocks of the lovely Esplanade, high on the edge of the Supai, there's a warm feeling inside, knowing that I've visited all those little canyons with the jewel names, another link in our repertoire of Canyon jaunts.

Dawn arrives on the piñon-covered Esplanade. A burst of orange treats us to a perfect sunrise on our last day. I sit on a big, flat boulder near our campsite and let it all sink in. Deep, shadowy Bass Canyon leading to the red Colorado River, the buttes, pinnacles, tremendous gorges, places unknown to humans which will never be reached in the foreseeable future. The miles and miles of Canyon with its hidden side canyons, gullies, mesas, will probably always remain wild except for a relatively small part. Wild, wonderful, austere. The adjectives go on and on. There's no way to capture it, only to feel it deep inside and live in its innermost parts for eleven days.

Breakfast is scanty and the packs will be light, as I stuff my filthy things in one last time. I walk over my shirt without a thought, a sure sign that cleanliness has ceased to exist. Murray has started up the trail and I take my last look at the Esplanade, heavily vegetated with piñon pine, oak, cliffroses, bright red paintbrush, purple and pink phlox and a few delicate blue flax for surprises. As the trail begins to climb through the Coconino Sandstone, it becomes very rocky and steep. Interesting to think that Bass used to bring his ore out on mules on this tricky route and, later, even tourists. Supposedly, Mrs. Bass would take a mule and her laundry from the rim to the river and return with clean clothes three days later, since there was no water on the rim where they lived. The Bass children, at very young ages, would also ride their horses up and down this trail and, surprisingly, lived to tell about it.

I climb higher and higher on this interesting trail and then, suddenly, I'm on the rim! Again, it feels good and also sad. The trip is over and I must start thinking of mundane things like cars, money, houses, laundry, etc. That world has been gone for eleven days. But coming out of the Canyon at Bass Trailhead is good. Nobody is here, no crowds of gaping tourists clicking shutters. The shock at other trailheads is too great. One must come back gradually and the thirty-mile trip on a dirt road to the main tourist area will give us a chance to acclimate slowly.

Once again I seek out my throne on the rocks. The VW bus has a flat, so after a heavenly treat of an orange left in the bus, Randy and Murray deal with that problem while I take my last look. The swifts are dive-bombing as I say one last good-bye to Bass Canyon and all those other hidden canyons which hosted us.

The tire is fixed and we bounce along the rutted, dirt road through plateaus of sagebrush and piñon pine, still with our hearts and minds in the Canyon. Eleven days, seeing almost no one, sleeping under the stars and moon, cooking on a tiny stove, searching for and purifying small amounts of precious water, walking, climbing, over fifty miles, listening to the frogs and crickets, and then being overwhelmed by the silence of the desert. Going to sleep as the stars emerge, getting up before the sun, always in tune with nature's rhythm.

Our thoughts are jolted as we realize we are on the paved road of the South Rim Drive. Automobiles are roaring past, cameras are clicking, people of all nationalities are running or walking to the edge for "the look." Rim shock! It insults our minds, our bodies, our mellow state. In a fog, we get a site at Mather Campground, get the clothes washed, and scrub our own grimy bodies in the welcome shower. Slowly we emerge from our confused mood, helped by the civilized pleasures of soap, hot water, and iced tea.

But the shock lingers. One must ease into this scene more slowly and it really just can't be done. To walk out of the mystical Grand Canyon after a long trip and be confronted with an alien world of noise, confusion, and hordes of people is too great a contrast.

We put on clean clothes and follow our established tradition with dinner at El Tovar. The Margaritas are delicious and the chilled salad forks arrive in their red, folded napkins, as the waiter, with the black suit and white, ruffled shirt, bows properly and the candlelight glimmers on our tan faces. It's all there as before, a proper ending to a wonderful trip.

CHAPTER 8

The Tough One

North Bass • October 1985

The last golden rays of a North Rim sunset leaves Swamp Point in radiance. We are camped here at the point and tomorrow begins another journey into the depths of this special place. Randy, Murray and I are going to try for the second time to do the North Bass Trail, which the guidebooks warn is only for the most experienced hikers in the best of shape.

A year ago, going down the extremely steep talus after a rain, Murray stepped on an unstable rock and fell, pulling a muscle in his leg, which prevented him from going downhill but not up. We camped only one night and the next day went back up to the Muav Saddle, which links Swamp Point and the isolated Powell Plateau, about 800 feet below the rim. Here the little CCC cabin, circa 1932, is located. Murray insisted that he was fine and would stay in the cabin, so Randy and I went up to Powell Plateau for an overnight. This proved to be a real treat and a place we probably never would have visited otherwise. So once again we will try the North Bass.

Swamp Point is twenty miles on a dirt road off the main North Rim road and is the trailhead for North Bass. It is very quiet here this late afternoon. A few cars are parked in the bushes. A couple of backpackers come out, after having spent ten days in the Canyon, with that happy, satisfied glow on their tanned faces. One young fellow comes up the trail and walks by without a word. We understand.

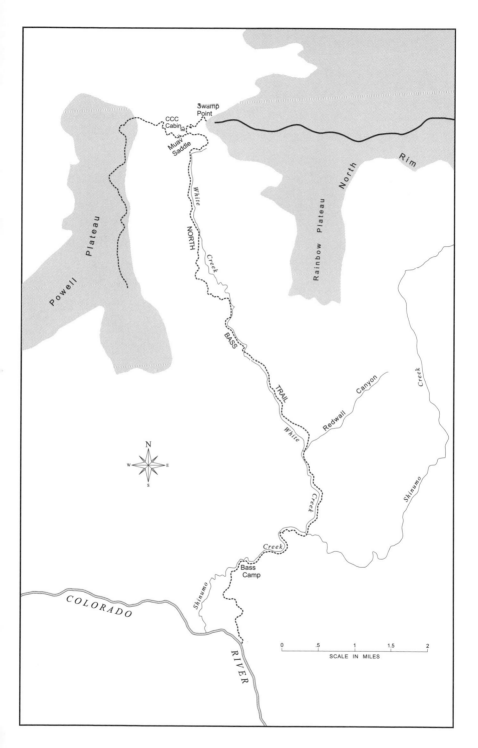

Swamp
Point

CCC
Cabin

Muav
Saddle

White

NORTH

Creek

BASS

TRAIL

White

Redwall   Canyon

Creek

Shinumo

Creek

Powell

Plateau

Rainbow Plateau

North

Rim

N
W   E
S

Creek

Bass
Camp

Shinumo

COLORADO

RIVER

0   .5   1   1.5   2
SCALE IN MILES

105

FIRST DAY

Acool morning greets us. Our packs are fat and heavy, every pocket zipper is bulging. There's a delicate glow as the early sun illuminates the gold and red oak which edge the Canyon rim. The dark depths of North Bass look uninviting at the moment. The vegetation is thick on the North Rim, since its annual rainfall is twenty-five inches and all of it funnels down the southward-sloping plateau into the Canyon, carving steep-sided gorges, one of which we are about to enter. Now comes that feeling of anticipation, a little concern, wondering if Murray and I are getting too old for this crazy sort of thing. But we are determined to continue hiking the Canyon and Randy, praise be, is willing to come along, which is always a good feeling.

Fourteen miles to the river, but tonight we'll camp halfway. Murray heads down the trail as Randy and I close up the two VW buses. On goes the old, familiar, blue pack, groaning with food, clothing and sundry items. My blue house is essential, but I wish right now that it were on wheels or on the back of a llama. The first part of the trail down to the Muav Saddle is a pleasant walk. The oak are brilliant red and orange. Nothing wrong with this sparkling morning except the helicopters and planes roaring below the rim and through the Muav Saddle. What an infringement on a wilderness experience! Who has the greater right, those who come from all over the world to hike and enjoy the solitude of the Canyon, or a few commercial outfits who make money taking the affluent for a quick ride? It's going to soon be decided how to accommodate both, after public hearings are conducted by the Park Service. But no politics now!

Murray is waiting at the saddle. We check out the little Civilian Conservation Corps cabin and head back to the trail.

"Rocky slopes with extreme difficulty," as quoted in the guidebook, await us. Down the steep talus slope, watching each footstep, trying to avoid loose rocks and looking for quick handholds on nearby bushes. Past the steepest part and now come the scratches, with every conceivable desert bush reaching out with claws and tentacles for bare legs and arms. Then overhanging branches grab the top of my pack, stopping me abruptly. Tiring business, battling the lush vegetation of the North Rim trails. We reach the beginning of White Creek, a pleasant little stream meandering down to join Shinumo Creek and then on to the Colorado River. Still very brushy with all those lovely bushes blocking our way.

Murray passes his bad-memory spot as we make our way along the trail. We cross the creek in the little hollow and, as I step on a large rock that looks deceptively solid, I find myself being carried by my heavy pack down into the stream. My elbow smacks against something unforgiving and I'm trapped in brush like a turtle on his back. Murray frees me by unfastening the buckle on my pack. I survey the damage, a bloody ankle and elbow, both of which still seem to be in working order. White Creek is soothing, as I sit and soak my injured parts. Is there bad karma for us on this trail?

Back on the trail. I won't let North Bass have the last word. A wet towel and ace bandage around my ankle and a wet sleeve for my elbow dull the pain. Going is slow, up and over deep ravines with the usual battle of the bushes. Finally we reach the top of the Redwall and, like all the openings in that giant border of limestone throughout most of the Canyon, it is always steep and rough. My knees and legs are no longer working efficiently. It's almost five o'clock and it's been a very long day. At last we are down. There's only a little level ground deep in this gorge, but there is water up the small canyon, so it's home for tonight. We finish dinner in the early darkness and now at last it's been worth the struggle as I stretch out under the stars for a welcome twelve-hour snooze.

SECOND DAY

It's a warm and pleasant morning at 7:00 A.M. in this tiny, boxed-in slash right below the Redwall. I bend my ankle and elbow cautiously. Things work better once I'm up and moving. The trail begins in a dry creekbed, with a large obstacle of boulders greeting us immediately as we leave camp. There is no way down for us two aging hikers without lowering our packs. Without those ridiculous encumbrances, I'm agile and feel almost youthful, but put on close to fifty pounds and I'm a clumsy, ponderous creature climbing over large boulders and letting myself down to more boulders. But it's all part of backpacking and no one is making me do it. The day continues with more scrambling over formidable hunks of rock, around charming pools of water, hot sun blasting down as we dunk our hats in them for relief. We seek our lunch-time shade, where giant wasps with much authority mix with huge black-and-orange tarantula hawks, all busy on a nearby flowering bush.

Many stops for shade and water before we finally reach Redwall Canyon, after a short detour above the famous Butchart Chockstone, which we can look down upon through a narrow slash in the rock. We descend a steep, little canyon as Randy looks up from a shady spot below. Once more we lower our packs down to his waiting arms and then lower ourselves to join him in a shadowy, cool nook in this small crevasse. Again we detour, this time to look up at the giant chockstone which is wedged in a slot of vertical walls, covered with maidenhair fern, framed by the blue sky high above. As we relish the shade and cooling water, three Utah fellows come up the trail. Nice visit about Canyon experiences and then they head up and we go down. A fine walk through cool stream water, surrounded by high walls on either side. A few red monkeyflowers cling to the rocky sides.

Once more the boulders begin and the detours around deep pools, with long chutes down slick rock, which would be wonderful fun without packs. Randy is called upon a couple of times again when packs must be lowered. We are looking for the confluence of White and Shinumo creeks, our destination tonight. More sinuosities ahead before we spot Randy, who has found an excellent campsite. Shinumo is a small river lined with tamarisks and cottonwoods. That heavenly cool water! Murray plops himself in totally as I soak my hot feet and splash its soothing wetness over my body. Ah, water, clean bodies. Soup and beans for dinner by candle lantern while crickets serenade. Absolute bliss! Randy is occupied and intrigued by a neighboring ant colony. The ant hole is open until evening and then it closes, leaving a few ants outside as guards or late stragglers, who didn't get home before the hole closed. But I'm home and ready to close myself in for the night in my red, down bag.

THIRD DAY

We all agree at breakfast that this spot at the confluence is too pleasant to leave, so we decide to spend another night here instead of making our way up Shinumo Creek to find another campsite. The sun is in and out so we rig up the tarp between the willows and the

cottonwoods to cre-
ate a little cabana be-
side the beautiful
creek. Randy is
stretched out on his
pad, sound asleep
and oblivious of the
flies which feast on
the bloody gashes on
his legs. Murray is in
a dream-like mood
and I write down
these profound
words in rhythm

Canyon Wren

with the bubbling flow of the water. Two water ouzels play
hide-and-seek while a canyon wren darts in and out of the
willows. No one has come by today. Now and then a spatter
of rain hits the tarp. A wonderful, lazy day and especially
nice for my black-and-blue, battered body.

The sun is getting lower and we become energized.
Randy hikes up Shinumo Creek. Murray and I go downstream and think we spot some very crumbled Anasazi ruins
across the creek. It's hard to tell for sure, but there is an indefinite, little doorway still visible. The ancient ones, the
Anasazis, did live in this lush canyon and what a natural
choice. Lots of clear water to grow their beans, corn and
squash. Randy returns to camp saying that upper Shinumo
is a jungle, with very few camping spots. Threatening clouds
convince us to put up the tents, but we'll sleep out until the
first raindrops fall.

Today's destination is the Colorado River, the creator of the Grand Canyon, with its slow, cutting force carving its way through the centuries. Nice hiking along the creek and then right through it, with three crossings, boots and all. Murray and I can't manage the jumps and balancing acts of my son to get across, so we just wade in. Feels good and squishy in my wet boots. We round a curve and there sits Randy in William Bass's old camp, greeting us with Bass's old coffeepot. An array of broken, purple and turquoise bottles, rusty tools, gold-panning equipment are all spread out. A weathered sign, neatly printed, left over from his garden, says "tomatoes". Bass was given six months to live, moved to the Grand Canyon and lived another forty years. He eventually saw the profit in tourism and began to bring a few hardy souls down the steep trail from the South Rim on mules and then across the river in his homemade cable car; they camped here, partway up Shinumo Creek. He even provided fresh vegetables from his lush garden for his guests.

Now we must climb about 500 feet to a ridge and then down the other side, where the river suddenly appears, a strange olive-green color reflected in the bright sunshine. A hot trip down to the distant white beach. A large tamarisk welcomes us with shade for lunch as we wiggle our toes in the white sand. A tasty pasta salad is concocted from leftover spaghetti, parsley, sprouts, and a can of mustard sardines. Randy has a portable icebox to keep our greens fresh — a wet dishcloth wrapped around them and kept moist during the day. We have even been known to carry alfalfa seeds in water in a plastic jar and sprout them along the way. Works fine, and what a treat!

I do my laundry in the green river, launder myself and dry all on the warm rocks. Quickly the river begins to rise and the rocks disappear, so I head for higher ground. No longer a wild river, it is now controlled by humans in an office in Montrose, Colorado, pushing buttons, answering the need for power in the big cities of the Southwest.

I watch the flowing water from my prone position, my head propped on a rolled-up sleeping bag, when suddenly a raft appears and then another and another and still another — horror of horrors! The come in for a landing. The spell is broken, our Robinson Crusoe beach is being overrun with young, brightly-clad bodies. Two of the bodies come running up to us and say they hope they'll not disturb us. It turns out to be a boat company's "employee after-the-season trip." What can we say? It's not our private beach. So we sit, three haughty and judgmental backpackers watching in great disdain as out come the beach paraphernalia, including a "boom box" which immediately cracks the peace and quiet with ear-shattering sounds.

We are invited for dinner. We are trapped, there is no place else to go so late in the day, so we meekly accept and join them for dinner. How strange to hear an electric blender, powered by a small generator, making Margaritas in the bottom o the Grand Canyon! To a backpacker this is sacrilege. We eat a Mexican dinner and I even indulge in a Margarita, feeling like a traitor. Then, like fish out of water, we pay our respects and disappear into the dark to our campsite. The party noise level increases — yelling, dancing and laughter as a huge bonfire lights up the beach. Fun and games and noise. The sound of the river is gone, the brilliance of the stars can't compete with the giant fire and the spell of the Canyon is broken, at least for us. I try to sleep between bursts of merrymaking, but it's impossible. Finally all that energy wears down and, as the bonfire becomes just glowing embers, peace once more returns and we have our private beach back again.

We had planned to stay two nights by the river, but so has the beach party. We must move on. The "boom box" is playing, the boat people are milling around deciding whether to play Trivia or go for a hike. Suddenly our tolerance level snaps and we rush to get away. Randy takes off muttering, "Boot culture and boat culture don't mix." Hiking up the steep trail, only a few minutes from the beach, I take one last look at the colorful, little boat creatures as they are suddenly swallowed up in the immensity and grandeur of the Canyon. Mere tiny specks on their frantic merry-go-round of life, trying to drown out the natural sounds of the earth, the flow of the river, the call of the raven. Silence and solitude can be threatening to some folks. But now as I sit high above the river on this cool, cloudy day, the Canyon spell weaves its magic once more and life is in balance again. All just a reminder to us humans that our time on this earth is but a split second and it is pretty silly to stand in judgment or feel superior to other human critters, when peace and solitude are only a few dozen footsteps away in this vast land.

Lunch at our old campsite at the confluence before we start the long, arduous twelve miles to the rim. We enter boulder-strewn White Creek, always searching for the easiest way among those immense piles of rock, trying to avoid the beautiful, little pools. Finally I give in and walk through the water, not caring if my boots stay dry. Up and over some black ledges where years ago someone, perhaps a miner, thoughtfully imbedded an iron rod to help our scrambling.

Murray and Randy are somewhere behind me as I meet two men who had decided to give up going any further until they saw this not very young lady who claimed she'd been to the river and back. I convince them that it isn't all that bad and they go for their packs and head down.

We reach the chockstone sculpture as the packs get hoisted up again. Then up and back to the riverbed again. Weariness is setting in. The creek is still dry, so no stopping until the water begins again. Seems a long time since we left the big river this morning. Lots of elevation gain, but the most tiring of all is the constant balancing act from one boulder to another and then the climb up and over these ancient fellows. There's never a moment to just let your feet carry you along — it's continual watching from step to step.

Cheers! The creek water has reappeared and we follow it along until we find some rock slabs flat enough to camp upon. It's overcast and threatening, so up go the tents. The stars come out and then disappear. It's been a long day as my weary bones and muscles sink into that great invention, the self-inflating pad.

SIXTH DAY

The agreeable sound of gentle White Creek pouring over the ledges of slickrock awakens me to a cloudy morning. Now and then a blue patch of sky appears, only to quickly fade behind the fast moving clouds. Pleasant hiking temperature but I miss the sun to cheer us on the long day ahead. More streamed walking and boulder climbing.

We meet a group from San Francisco, including some "first time" Canyon hikers. Part of the party has bogged down and can go no further. A rough trip for novices. They would have been happier on the Bright Angel Trail for their first Grand Canyon experience.

Now comes the Redwall ascent. It was a nightmare going down that first day, since I was tired and sore and the hour was late. So going up is definitely easier and also less stressful. You can only fall on your face, unless you are very clumsy and topple off the edge or go over backward. But it is still up, up, up, grabbing onto the obliging manzanita branches. I've changed my mind about wanting sunshine. I'm dripping with sweat, even under the somber, grey sky. Quite an amazing trail, twisting and switchbacking between the scratchy vegetation and following along the cliffs. I was never quite sure when the top of the Redwall was reached, but it's no longer steep as my feet wend their way through the mesquite and manzanita, following erratic cairns.

Randy is far ahead somewhere in the maze of brush and gullies. Murray and I have apparently missed an all-knowing cairn and realize, when Randy shouts across the gully, that we are headed down the wrong way. We retrace our steps, follow another misplaced cairn, but the third time, of course, is a charm and we seem to be headed correctly down an amazingly steep hillside to the gully below. We stop for a much needed drink and claw our way, almost on hands and knees, up the next hillside. Three gullies to go up and over before we reach the big ponderosa where we plan to camp tonight. In and out of the thorny snags that reach out from above and the flesh-slashing branches of the long stemmed yucca which lie in wait at leg level. The wind begins and then the rain. Murray's bad knee, a result of an ancient ski injury, is tiring out and our pace is slow. We put on rain gear and continue on the vague trail with its unreliable cairns, and finally reach White Creek. In the distance we can see the tall, lone ponderosa pine down in the creekbed, a beacon of hope.

Yucca

Randy is setting up his tent as we at last reach our destination. There is no water right here, but about a quarter-mile up, the stream begins again. I offer to get the water. I find a small, clear pool, line up the pots, pans, bottles and gratefully plop myself down among the soft grasses and begin the meditative process of pumping away the impurities, if any, of White Creek with our wonderful little filter pump. I stare at the minute creatures going about their business underwater. Red and yellow leaves float over the quiet water as I slowly pump, in and out, in and out.

I return to camp just as the rain lets loose. It's dinner in the tents tonight, with a carefully balanced candle lantern to eat by. We all look like rodents in their holes as we peer out of tent openings for conversation. Dirty pots and pans are left out for the rain to wash and I crawl into my red cocoon and watch the clouds move across the ominous sky, opening up dark slots where stars are hiding. Unconsciousness takes over until I feel drops on my face. I zip up the rain fly and settle down for the night with raindrops on the nylon roof.

A steady rain is falling on a very wet world outside the tents and, at this higher elevation, the thermometer reads a cool forty-one degrees. The rain continues to pour down, so we burrow back into our dens, eat some breakfast, always checking for that hopeful patch of blue that never comes. Murray and I vow that at the next letup, we'll go for it. This is it! Down come the soggy, dripping and heavier tents. We roll up the messy things, stuff our packs as quickly as possible and leave Randy, looking like an owl, peering out of his hole. White Creek is now a full-fledged stream. There is water above us, below us, and a lot coming in at the edges. Every tree and bush we brush against lets loose another downpour. We pick our slippery way up and over the ubiquitous rockpiles, and now the big grunt begins up to the Muav Saddle. Abruptly the rain ends and there is a burst of sunshine. It is so welcome! We are soaked, inside and out. My wet wool hat and gloves have a dank, sheep aroma. We snack and spread out to dry as Randy catches up, looking like the proverbial drowned rat.

Now comes the trek up the very steep talus slope, with slippery patches of mud sending us sliding backwards instead of upwards. Again the faithful manzanita, with their beautiful, bright rust and somber grey, twisted branches, provide handholds and pull-ups. At last the white wall of the Coconino Sandstone appears and I'm on more level ground. The little cabin is our lunch stop. This one-room cabin was built in the thirties by the CCC, along with some of the maintained trails in the Canyon. This program provided work in the depression years for hundreds of young men and today it's providing us with shelter from the intermittent showers which have begun again.

We dump our soggy clothes on the floor, looking in our packs for something dry. The only thing that qualifies is my down parka, which is tucked in the very bottom in a water-proof bag. Everything else is soaked. The weather alternates between bursts of sun and dark clouds. When the sun does appear, we rush outside to dry out wet clothes, only to have the clouds move in again. Back into the cabin where it's very cold. I cook up some hot soup on our little gas stove. An old, wood-burning stove is in the cabin, but fires are not allowed in the Canyon so we huddle on the mouse-eaten mattresses and decide what to do next. The plan was to go to Powell Plateau, but our spirits are a bit dampened along with every-thing else. If only the sun would stay out in earnest so we could dry things out.

Finally the thought of cold, wet sleeping bags is too much and we unanimously decide that we have survived the North Bass and we are willing and very ready to head up to Swamp Point. Another consideration is the twenty-mile dirt road to the highway. With rain or snow it could be questionable, to say the least. We're cutting the trip three days short, but we're satisfied and Powell Plateau will have to wait for us to return later and walk through its majestic ponderosas, looking for Indian ruins.

Another forty-five minutes of up, but now it's a normal trail, with long views into Bass Canyon. Brilliant splashes of reds and golds turn the landscape into a tapestry of fall col-ors. The down parka comes off and my fingers have come back to life as the sun peeks out once more, bathing the land with a warm, golden glow, while low, foggy, white clouds boil up from the depths below.

One last step and the trip is over. The VWs are patiently waiting for their owners. Again the dichotomy of feelings, glad I did it and sad to have it end. Randy joins me and we toast our adventures with the traditional cold beer. Our threesome stands quietly looking down into that mystical den in our earth called the Grand Canyon, marveling at its power and allure that keeps bringing us back, time after time.

We load the wet packs into the buses and begin the slow trip to the highway. A covering of snow makes it look very wintery as we slide along the muddy road. The fog is thick as we approach the North Rim Lodge. We decide to splurge and stay in a cabin, rather than camp. After hot showers, and with dry, clean clothes, we enter civilization and the dining room. Never the degree of "rim shock" on the North Rim as on the South—less frantic activity.

The old lodge is quiet and pleasant, with its high, dark, beamed ceiling and tall windows looking out at the now foggy, dark Canyon. No chilled forks here, as in the fancy bistros of the South Rim, just a relaxed place to have our usual end-of-trip dinner. As the candles flicker we top off our meal with chocolate sundaes and talk about the trip. The North Bass was not an easy one, we all agree, but at least we have done it. As always, the good parts outweigh the bad and it all adds up to knowing the Grand Canyon just a little better and exploring one more of its hidden corners.

As we leave the handsome, old lodge for our warm cabin, the cold fog wraps around us and I have a secure and happy feeling, knowing I have added a few more memories to my file.

CHAPTER 9

Back Again in the Canyon

Deer Creek to Thunder River • September/October 1991

A six-year gap existed without any Grand Canyon trips. Southern Utah's incredible canyon country kept us busy exploring its mesas and slot canyons and working for its Wilderness designation and preservation. But the magical pull of the Grand Canyon finally led us back in 1991 to repeat an old favorite with variations. Unfortunately, Murray was unable to go, his last trip being the North Bass at the age of 71.

Rain has been falling at the North Rim for the past day — heavy at times as the clouds hang low over the rim and down into the canyon. Travelers who have come to the North Rim of the Grand Canyon restlessly wander about, competing for the limited comfortable chairs in the lodge, waiting impatiently for the skies to clear. Hikers and backpackers along with tour bus folks thumb through paperbacks, glancing now and then through the tall windows to see if the weather is improving.

Randy and I have a date to enter the Grand Canyon beginning tomorrow morning. We have a backcountry permit for a six-day trip from Deer Creek to Thunder River and we are ready and anxious to leave.

FIRST DAY

Morning dawns in the campground. The clouds are there, but the rain has stopped. Our packs are filled and waiting and the damp campground is still asleep as we pull out to the main road and head for the dirt road, 20 miles to Monument Point, our trailhead destination. The sky seems to be clearing as we make our way along the back roads of the North Rim. Golden aspen trees outshine the deep forest green of the conifers as a weak morning sun drifts through the forest.

Monument Point has more cars than we have seen in the past. Several rather aging gentlemen are putting on their packs. One leaves, loaded with gear, sneakers dangling from his pack. Randy is still adding things to his pack, so I leave and head for the rim, walking through the fall colors of oak. I catch up with the two middle-aged guys, visit a bit and muse over the pack that one is carrying. It sags off his shoulder, various items fastened by strands of rope flop back and forth. He looks quite miserable and he has only gone less than a mile on relatively flat ground. He is overweight and would probably be more at home walking his dog in the park. I wonder if he knows what is ahead.

Randy has not yet arrived so I start down the steep slope, the typical Grand Canyon entrance to all backpacking trails—loose rocks, slippery shale and precipitous drop-offs at each switchback. I follow the two gentlemen, holding my breath as they stumble and almost fall. Finally, as the fat fellow's pack swings and sways dangerously from side to side, I feel compelled to speak, telling him to tighten up the shoulder stabilizers, which he was unaware existed. With that advice, I head down the trail, wondering how far they will make it.

Randy has caught up with me at a beautiful viewpoint. The mysterious and breathtaking panorama of the Grand Canyon stretches below us, always sending a rush of emotion over me. It's been six years since we have hiked off the North Rim and we have done this trail twice before, but this time we will vary it with a route along the river.

The steepness of the trail continues, at last giving way to the inviting Esplanade, where the potholes are filled with rain water and are as blue as the sky above. The weather has become ideal, clear and not too warm. Thunderheads are in the distance with sheets of rain touching the horizon here and there.

Down the Redwall, an easy one as descents through the Redwall go. Lunch is eaten under a giant slab of rock, as the temperature begins to rise. The view is down into Surprise Valley, and I remember that scary day years ago that the temperature reached 115 degrees and I almost didn't leave Surprise Valley.

Randy decides on a short nap under his cool rock slab, so I leave him and go down the remainder of the Redwall trail. As I hike along with my mind on nothing in particular, I am rudely brought to attention by the terrifying pressure cooker sound of the western rattler, who is suddenly blocking the trail immediately in front of me. With body arched and rattles in full action, I obligingly stop while adrenaline shoots through me. To go around him requires some unwanted maneuvering through boulders, so I throw small pebbles and bang my walking stick until he gives up and heads under a nearby rock. I worry about Randy so I leave a note on the trail and quickly go by Mr. Rattler's hideout while he rattles me a noisy farewell.

Into Surprise Valley and the best surprise is that the clouds are keeping the temperature tolerable. Randy arrives as I sip on my water bottle. He found the snake still lying under the rock. We know that rattlers are throughout the Canyon, probably under many of the rocks we pass, but meeting one is always an event.

Another couple hours of rough hiking and then the steep descent into Deer Creek, our destination for tonight. The sun has come out and it's very hot. I am beginning to wilt a bit, the day has suddenly become very long and the eleven miles from rim to campsite seems more like twenty.

Randy has disappeared , but I find his pack on the trail and then I hear the sound of rushing water. I gratefully drop my pack to follow that delightful sound. There, out of the high rock walls of this inferno bursts precious water! A pool lined with maidenhair fern and watercress lies at the bottom of these amazing falls. The Canyon reward for weary and hot backpackers! I drink the pure spring water and dunk my blazing head in its cool gift of life. We nibble on watercress and let the spray drift over our sticky bodies. Must I leave this oasis?

Reality tells me that we still have a ways to go to Deer Creek, so I force myself up the trail and back to the pack. Down the trail again and at last we are home for the night. Cottonwoods with the first blush of fall, prickly pear cactus heavy with purple fruit line our campsite, and nearby Deer Creek flows cheerfully by. Dinner is always special the first night, tasting so good for tired bodies. But always the best part is when the sleeping bag is unrolled and sore muscles sink into the accommodating inflatable pad and the day comes to an end under the sparkling Milky Way.

SECOND DAY

Twelve hours of sleep have left us refreshed and ready for a new day. The sky is clear. I look forward to a day without my house on my back as we go downstream to find another campsite for tonight. Food is hung, packs are tucked in the shade of the cottonwoods and we slip through the narrows leading to Deer Falls and the Colorado River. The long slot of convoluted rock, sculptured by the centuries, is beautiful. The twists and turns drop deeply as Deer Creek finds its way to the river.

Out into the sun. It's going to be a hot one today. A chuckwalla sits on a rock with its baggy skin soaking up the heat. Looking down at the river, there are several rafts and kayaks. We will not be alone. As we round the last switchback, the roar of Deer Falls fills the silence, dropping a hundred feet over the red rock into a deep pool. The spray fills the air with instant air conditioning. Lots of activity at the beach. Boat people, who now become hikers, are headed to the falls and the narrows. We seek out a shady spot under the tamarisks and spend the day watching the scene as boatloads of people come and go. As we munch on dried lunch fare, I feel like an ostracized aborigine while the boat people set up a table filled with its array of fresh vegetables, sliced meats, jars of mayonnaise, mustard and all the trimmings, cold beer included.

The hours pass by, the river casts its spell. Blue-green water rolls over smooth rocks, then becomes frothy white as the rapids form. Two orange butterflies play tag. Randy dozes as the shadows begin to lengthen on the high Canyon walls.

The falls send a farewell spray for the hot steep climb up from the river. Back through the dark, cool narrows. The boat people have ropes and are playing down in the bottom, their voices echoing back and forth. Quite a few people in a Sierra Club group are headed for Deer Creek. Too many for our tastes. Four pleasant guys are camped very close to us. They have come via the river route which we will take tomorrow. Good to hear about it firsthand. Fall's early darkness lures us into bed after we have enjoyed the evening.

I t's 5:00 A.M. and very dark. The campers next to us quietly fumble around with flashlights, packing up for their hike to the Esplanade. We also pack up, holding our flashlights in our mouths as we fit the belongings into the packs. At 6:00 it's light enough to leave and we are on our way to the river route leading to Tapeats Creek and Thunder River.

Breakfast in the cool of the morning on the saddle. The distant cliffs are turning that familiar rosy pink, and down in the shady depths of verdant Deer Creek can be seen two tiny blue tents under the cottonwoods.

I leave Randy brushing his teeth and make my way over the Tonto-like trail. A whitetail deer disappears in the distance and a baby snake slithers across the ground. Randy appears with the first view of the river below, sparkling like silver as it zigzags its way through the somber cliffs of Granite Narrows. The trail continues, in and out of small dry washes, high above the river and then it begins to drop, drop, down and down. We meet another Sierra Club group who tell us they had to use ropes at Bonita Creek. But we are going up which should be easier, I tell myself. Those telltale butterflies are always there when I'm about to face an unknown route. And there's something about being seventy-one that reminds me that maybe I'm not as agile as I used to be. But Randy is great, never makes me feel like he's impatient. He has to feel it, though, as I lumber along the trail while he could be flying along in his fleet-footed way.

The beach stretches before us with its smooth sand and endless array of big and little boulders. It's hot! Shirts and hats are dunked in the cold Colorado River. We sit on the wet sand eating snacks. The boulder hopping continues, balancing on the black Vishnu Schist rocks, very old and very hot. Then there are the slippery, varnished hunks of river rocks and big, flat slabs of rough rock—I like those best. Randy is way ahead, of course, waiting for mom. That's okay, though, I used to do a lot of waiting for him in those growing-up years.

We are at Bonita Creek! There's, of course, no creek, only a wall of dark rock going straight up to somewhere. Randy negotiates it, heavy pack and all, without a second thought, leaves his pack at the top and comes back for mine. Easy and really kind of fun without that thing on my back, with hand-holds to pull up a reluctant body, footholds to balance on, and suddenly I'm on the top. We look down on what the backcountry information calls very steep and precarious. Doesn't take but a few minutes, but going down could be a nightmare without ropes to lower packs.

We drop once again to the river, cooling off in its cold waters. Then more rocks and boulder hopping and we are at Tapeats Creek. Next surprise of the day—Tapeats Creek looks like a river to me. It's fast, swift and wide as it spills into the Colorado River. I make good use of my trusty ski pole and manage to cross it without being washed into the Colorado.

Lunch is eaten under the shade of a giant boulder. A kayaker slips into the shore. I tell him how beautiful and graceful he and his kayak look, as they dart in and out of the frothy rapids and then join the rhythm and flow of the river. One of those fun things I never learned to do. Randy comments that no one has ever called a backpacker, picking his way down a steep trail, "beautiful"!

It's 12:30 P.M. and becoming increasingly hot for the first day of October. I wash out my shirt and look for shade as the

Great Blue Heron

sun comes blasting around our lunch rock. Randy has found some dense tamarisks where he'll no doubt sleep away the afternoon. I try under the willows, but they let in too much sun and are covered with bees. Looks like a long hot afternoon until I spy a rocky overhang just above the beach. I clamber up and here I am, two hours later, in a delightful shady alcove, looking out over the river and the scorching beach below. A little Anasazi-type cliff dwelling, no bees, no flies, only a tiny lizard checking me out. Spoke too soon, a red ant just stung me!

The sun finally leaves the beach, resting on the surrounding cliffs with a vermillion glow. Looks like we have the place to ourselves which is a real treat. Dinner is cooked with the river at our doorstep, while a great blue heron sits regally across the river looking for his dinner. October darkness closes in early and the little candle lantern casts a cheerful glow as we enjoy the coolness which has suddenly arrived.

A lazy awakening when a canyon wren gives her little song, certainly not the full spring repertoire, but always a welcome canyon sound. A lone bat is still searching for bugs before heading for bed. Cool greys, tans and subdued greens are reflected in the smooth section of the river, but in the rapids the tops of the waves are touched with rosy orange, reflected from the highest sun-drenched pinnacles. Two shiny black ravens swoop overhead with raucous chatter.

Today we head up Tapeats Creek. Supposedly only three miles, but not the three miles I often walk on East Sopris Creek Road in 50 minutes. We start up a rocky, talus slope, very steep, (how often do I repeat that description?), with ledges that stretch legs and test balance, then down the other side, reaching beautiful Tapeats Creek again. It's definitely a cascading and full-fledged river in my estimation. It is also a lush canyon with red monkeyflowers still blooming along the shoreline, big cottonwood trees, willows and redbud trees fed by the perennial water of Tapeats. Prickly pear cacti grow in abundance, mixed in with almost tropical vegetation. What a contrast!

Just as I had relaxed into this pleasant, green world I'm faced with a 'little Bonita' wall that I must somehow get up. As usual Randy solves the crisis as I lift up my pack, camera and water bottle, leaving me free to do a little rock climbing. More walking along the water's edge through a jungle of horsehair grass and other thick vegetation. The trail stops abruptly and it's time for another river crossing. It's fast and deep. I stumble my way across trying to find safe places to put my feet instead of on slippery hidden rocks. Water oozes out of my boots and cools my feet as I reach shore. More

walking up and down rocky slopes and more river crossings. I'm getting better since I've learned to face my feet up
or downstream rather than let the current hit my feet sideways. But the water is also getting deeper in spots, up to my
crotch in fact.

Finally, we reach the confluence of Thunder River and
Tapeats Creek. I wade to shore and up a steep hillside where
the only convenient handhold is blocked by an old prickly
pear cactus Not something you want to cling to. Managed to
get up without being gored. We decide to go up a ways
along the Thunder River Trail for lunch beside the lower
falls. The cool spray has lowered the temperature at least 20
degrees.

Home tonight is
Upper Tapeats Creek.
Camping spots are
minimal in this tight,
heavily vegetated can-
yon with its towering
red walls, but we
manage to find a spot
complete with an
overhang, a tiny
spring pouring off the
wall, nurturing the
ubiquitous maiden-
hair fern alongside.

Bat

So here I sit, writing these rambling notes, on a big tilt-
ing boulder watching the sun send its late rays on the Canyon walls. The tops of the cottonwoods are golden green and
Tapeats Creek is blue-green topped with bubbling white as
it makes its way down to the Colorado River.

It's been an interesting day, not too many miles covered, but lovely scenery and a few challenges. Years ago, Murray, Randy and I brought Murray's daughter and her husband for part of this trip and they were not impressed. Couldn't wait to get out of this big hole called the Grand Canyon. In fact, several others we have introduced to this Canyon meandering have never wanted to return. The hiking is tough and the whole experience can be somewhat intimidating, but such mysterious and awesome beauty lies within its depths, that nothing else can quite compare!

FIFTH DAY

Late sun arrives in our "Anasazi" dwelling place. A warm night, but cool by the creek as I wash my face and greet the morning. The same azure blue sky fills the overhead slot. Randy will go up to the cave in Upper Tapeats Creek today. I'll go as far as I wish. It's a "be by oneself day". Randy leaves up the canyon. I do some washing, purify water, fuss around and finally decide to put on my boots and go upstream in spite of my dislike of stream crossings. I'm not about to sit here beside a red ant colony for five hours!

I pack a lunch and follow an indistinct trail which eventually turns into bushwhacking through heavy riparian growth. Up and down each side of the canyon. Still cool and in shadow. The first river crossing arrives and I survive nicely. The second one is swifter and scarier but the shore finally appears and I'm on the other side, scrambling over boulders. Enough of this, I don't seem to be getting anywhere. I find a huge, flat boulder, stretch out and settle in for a while. Time drifts by. I begin to hear voices. I sit up expecting to see hikers, but there is only blue sky, red rocks, quiet cottonwood leaves and the water rolling by. Perhaps I am having an Outward Bound experience, with only myself, no food, etc. But aha, I have last night's spaghetti, almonds and dried pineapple. I ought to survive just fine for a long time.

I would like to venture further but I am faced with a large boulder, dropping down to the creek with a stream crossing filled with deep holes and small rapids turning me into an instant chicken. I tell myself that water holds a certain fear for me because I never really learned to swim in arid Denver . Or maybe I am just a chicken!

Looks like the sun will never reach this canyon. I try to sketch the scene surrounding me, but as usual the Grand Canyon eludes me. I can't seem to do it. As one writer said, "The Canyon goes about its age-old business ignoring you completely." It's just too majestic, too mysterious to paint or capture with words. And yet I'll keep on trying out of sheer fascination.

It is almost noon and time for spaghetti. My rocky perch is cool, almost too cool with my wet socks on and no sun to dry them out. The voices continue, even thought I heard a dog bark. Upper Tapeats Canyon is classified "wild" where chances of human contact are minimal according to the Backcountry Office description. A real place to experience aloneness. So what am I experiencing on this beautiful October day in the depths of the Grand Canyon? A little uneasiness, I guess. River crossings, insects that sting and to which I react, snakes don't worry me much. I like being alone, it's different. Being alone in a wild primitive area puts an edge on things. I feel fortunate to be able to have this experience. How many people in this crowded world ever get such an opportunity? And most probably, don't want it either.

I decide to head downstream and back to the campsite. Randy said he would be back at 2:00 P.M. so we could head up to Thunder Falls, fill up on water for our dry camp in Surprise Valley tonight. I find myself looking at my watch. It's 1:30. Two o'clock arrives and then 2:30. My anxiety level is creeping up as the usual fears swirl around in my head. It's a rough canyon, deep pools and swift current in the stream, and what about Tapeats Cave? How far back would he go? I walk downstream and decide it's too early to be really concerned. What would I do if he didn't show up? The latest before I looked for help would be 4:00 P.M. And where would I find someone? It's dark by 6:00 now. I walk back up the trail trying not to imagine silly things. Then at 2:45 I see him coming into camp. Flashbacks overtake me, remembering when he and Cris Johnston, 10 and 12 years old, floated the Highline Canal in Denver and showed up two hours late. I wanted to spank and hug him all at the same time!

Two more river crossings and we are on the trail to Thunder Falls. Late afternoon shadows keep the switchbacks cool. On our right are the lower falls, cascading down the canyon walls leaving trails of greenery along the way. Now the big falls with spray filling the air. Almost too cool as we fill every bottle for our dry camp tonight and hike out tomorrow. I fill a cooking pot to rehydrate beans. Dried carrots go into a plastic bag filled with water. A funny sight as we trudge up the steep trail to Surprise Valley, a pot in one hand, my ski pole in another and Randy carefully carrying his pot. We reach the saddle, take our last look at Thunder Falls as it spouts out of the canyon wall, and turn our view into Surprise Valley, spread out below us as the setting sun leaves its last rosy tinge over all. The best campsite yet. Big smooth rocks here and there with wide spaces between the blackbrush for sleeping bags. We haven't had to use the tent on this trip. Only star-studded skies and a late moon every night. A gentle caressing warm breeze drifts over the valley as the Milky Way appears like a silver band across the sky.

SIXTH DAY

The last crescent of the old moon and a brilliant planet Venus below it are still in the dark sky as we break camp and try to beat the sun before it lands on the Redwall. A magical time for walking as the first desert pinks cover the landscape across Surprise Valley. Up the Redwall, reaching the top just as the sun reaches us. A spreading juniper provides breakfast shade with views back down into the valley. Four miles of Esplanade walking with endless views out to Kanab Creek, Indian Hollow, and on and on into the blue haze of unfamiliar mesas and horizons. Memories to file away in one's mind and to pull out whenever life gets bumpy. Potholes have all dried out since we were here six days ago. We find our water cache tucked into a juniper tree. Don't really need the water, but it's nice on a dirty face. Our final lunch is a lazy one, as we lie stretched out under a great, old, granddaddy juniper, munching on crackers, hummus, pineapple and the last granola bars.

The temperature has risen as midday finds us on the last steep pitch up the Coconino Sandstone to the rim. No shade as the sun beats directly on the trail. I look for lone trees along the way to hide under, drink my tepid water, wish for a warm breeze that comes and goes. This is definitely a long steep grunt to the top. Randy is of course ahead. Severe heat and I are not compatible. Now don't ask me why I keep coming back for more!

I must be three-fourths of the way up. No longer see Randy. My head is throbbing as sweat drips over my dark glasses. I round a switchback and there, sitting in the dirt under a deep overhang is a grinning Randy, cool as a cucumber, looking out over the canyon world below. I join him in the dirt and almost instantly I'm cool, as my dripping head and wet shirt begin to evaporate in the slight breeze. Incredible, another half-hour of this and I could be hyperthermic!

A few more switchbacks and there is the top of the North Rim. We have climbed 5,600 feet in addition to descending 5,600 feet. Another Grand Canyon experience fulfilled. Each time, especially as I get older and I finish a Canyon trip, my satisfaction is greater. Each backpack is always tough, and to realize I did it once more leaves me with a secret smugness. Will I do another one? Spring is a long ways off, but if history repeats itself

Utah Juniper

and if my sherpa is willing and available, I know that this intriguing and incredible gash in Mother Earth will pull me back and I will be unable to resist its mysterious call.

CHAPTER 10

A Final Journey

Tanner to Grandview • October 1992

FIRST DAY

Another Canyon trip? Didn't think it would happen this year, but here we are, Randy and I at Lipan Point parking lot at 6:30 A.M., ready for just one more Canyon trip. The deep blues and purples of that incredible hole in the earth are somber this cool morning on the South Rim of the Grand Canyon. But at 6:47 the sun rises and paints the highest pinnacles with warm red and pinks, awakening the Canyon to another morning.

We eat our breakfast in the Vanagon and I pack up last minute items into my pack. Randy still has major packing to do, as usual, so I'll start out first. No more stalling. Just thinking about any trip into the Canyon always creates a few goose bumps, and the older I get, the more goose bumps. But here I am, taking that first step down the rocky and steep Tanner Trail.

Very soon it all comes back and I'm in the familiar routine of slowly picking my way down, avoiding loose rocks and pebbles that could send me flying. Steep, steep is always the story of the beginning of any Canyon trip. The cool wind on the rim is gone as I peel off the wool sweater and get into the rhythm of the trail. I pass a man with older friends coming out. Nice to see my contemporaries doing crazy things too. Down through the rock slide, climbing over a jumble of

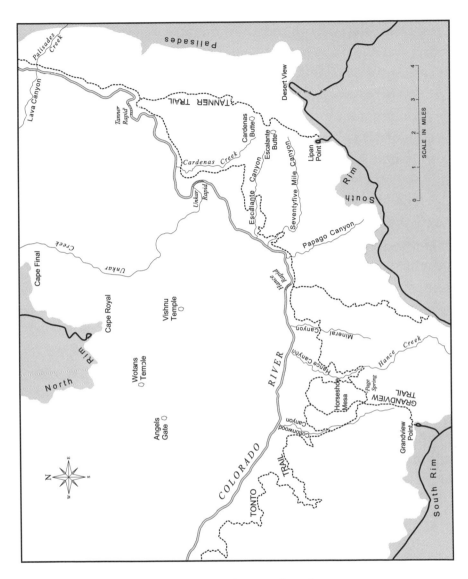

boulders and then out on a ridge with a fine view.

It's been an hour and a half since I left Randy at the rim. Decide to wait here until he shows up. Another half-hour slips by and the shade is cool, so I'll move on. At the end of the ridge it suddenly drops off abruptly. I can see the trail way below but how did I go astray? I've done the Tanner at least four times before so I should know where I am. Must retrace my steps back to the beginning of the ridge. Then I hear Randy call. He's down below on the trail. Obviously, I'm too high up, and then I see where I went wrong. Hikers, probably wanting to photograph a fine view, had made a well-worn trail out to the ridge and I dutifully followed it. Randy had been calling, but I figured it was simply the call of a raven. He's been in the Canyon too long! Or else I have.

The trail finally levels off a bit. Nice walking, but damn, this pack is heavy! We each have to carry a gallon of water, eight pounds, since the entire nine miles to Tanner is dry, all of which makes the house on my back quite miserable. The temperature is warming up, but there is still a welcome breeze. Lunchtime is under a large boulder. Placed in the far back is a coil of climbing rope. Wonder where the owner is? Hanging on a juniper tree and dancing in the breeze are white and black feathers attached to a leather cord. Interesting place with stories to tell that we'll never hear. A shiny black raven perches on the top branch of a dead juniper tree. He's definitely interested in our lunch menu, but patiently sits and watches as the sun turns his feathers into black patent leather. He croaks, guggles and entertains us with a full repertoire of strange and wonderful sounds. We leave this enchanted place with an offering of bread on a rock for Mr. Raven. He waits till we are well on our way before leaving his safe perch to pluck it up.

Raven

We have arrived at the Redwall, that ubiquitous band of limestone which always offers some steep, rocky conditions to the Canyon hiker. This is not the most difficult Redwall access in the Canyon, but it's shaley and steep, and my eyes stay glued to the trail beneath my feet. Now and then a stop to look below over the valley which seems quite green for this time of the year. We are off the Redwall, but not much improvement. Lots of down and it looks as though rockslides have eroded the trail. The early rains in the Canyon this spring closed both the North and South Kaibab trails because of rockslides. We are over halfway to our destination now but the river in the distance seems a continent away as it makes the big bend below Tanner Rapids.

The day is dragging on. My pack gets heavier and my feet get sorer with each mile we cover. The tantalizing blue river in the distance keeps me going, with help from a shot of ERG which is supposed to replenish the minerals and salts that run off my head and mess up my dark glasses, leaving the world looking watery and vague. We stop now and then and I gratefully take off the monster on my back. Getting it back on is even worse. I look for large rocks where I can prop it up and ease into it.

The Tanner Trail goes on and on, some of it steep and rocky and some pleasant and undulating over the red dox hills. The river doesn't seem to get much closer and it is already 4:00 P.M. I have been hiking since 8:30 A.M. and I'm definitely not breaking any speed records. At last, at 6:00 P.M. we are in the dry wash leading to the river. The old mesquite tree site where we have always camped has been closed for revegetation so we look for another. It's getting dark as we pick our way through the sand and river rocks looking for a spot for our two sleeping bags. Randy locates one in the evening gloom and I gratefully lower my pack for the final time today, spread out the tarp and rest my weary bones after Tanner's long nine miles. We light the candle lanterns and settle for cheese, crackers and soup since it is very dark by now. Randy's new candle lantern is very high-tech and makes my old Chinese-made one with the mica windows falling off look antique and inefficient.

The stars are out with the old familiar Milky Way right overhead. Almost too warm for a sleeping bag, but I crawl in and relish its unwashed comfort. No time for star gazing, just a goodnight to Murray back in old Snowmass as the sandman takes over my tired eyelids.

SECOND DAY

Morning on the rocky Tanner beach. My old knees and thighs are sore but functioning. The sun is still behind the cliffs and it's cool and pleasant as we munch on granola and Randy stews up his favorite prunes. How nice to know that it is only a little over three miles to our destination today.

As we walk high above the river, we can see some river rafters go by, their occupants soaking up the sun on the blue Colorado River. There's a feeling of that old desert heat as noon arrives under a clear blue sky. It's down to Cardenas for a lazy day to recoup our energy . We look for rocks along the way, a perfect one for Murray who has walked this trail before with us. Randy looks for a special one to take to Nepal in November. I find a nice little piece of twisted driftwood and two small rocks to bring to Murray as a memento. He did his last Canyon trip when he was 71 down the difficult North Bass Trail.

We find a small sandy beach set among coyote willows and tall tasseled grass. No shade, so we rig up a tarp with driftwood poles. River boats go by on this smooth stretch of river. I write as Randy naps under our Robinson Crusoe Ramada. A river boat stops and announces that a large group will be camping nearby. They are studying the flow level of the river as it leaves Glen Canyon Dam, and its effects on the beaches. Since the water released is controlled by computers in Montrose for the benefit of the growing populations of Arizona, California, etc. to provide power, there has been a pattern of high water and low water, destroying beaches and vegetation. The Grand Canyon Trust, a private group, has led the fight to change this pattern. An EIS is now being done and I guess this group is doing consulting work. They have camped on the other side of the tamarisks and we hardly know they are there except for two young women who are bathing in the 47-degree river, and actually seem to be enjoying it. Brrr.

It's 5:25 P.M. and the sun has disappeared behind the cliffs, but as usual has left behind its last rays turning the high cliffs into a brilliant, fiery finale of the day. The glow is reflected in the wide, quiet river, which is unusually clear. Randy has gone for a walk. We were invited to the neighbors for dinner, but darkness comes too early to go camp hopping. Besides, my dehydrated, homemade spaghetti sauce looks too tempting.

Just as we are finishing our gourmet meal, a late boat arrives in the darkness, part of the group. That could be a spooky trip on the river at night. The boatman must know the river well. Tonight is going to be cool. The Big Dipper is resting on the high dark cliffs, and as I look through the binoculars, stars are everywhere — the Milky Way is a sparkling band across the ebony sky. A coyote howls, a single wild call in the distant canyon. Nice way to end the day.

THIRD DAY

The river still casts a cool cover over our little beach. Sweats and sweaters feel good. The sun has a long road to travel to reach us in the bottom of the Grand Canyon at 7:00 A.M. in late October. Yoga for my still tender muscles and then hot oatmeal, fruit and tea. Today is a long haul to Escalante. We pack up. I walk through the tamarisks to find our boat neighbors and persuade them to carry out some trash which we cleaned up at our campsite. It's unusual to find trash in the Canyon, most hikers are responsible, but not these.

We are headed up to the Cockscomb, before dropping into Escalante Canyon and to the river again. Lots of up and also delightful Tonto-type walking. We are way above the river looking down on Unkar, which according to historians was a major Anasazi site. There is only a formation of large rocks left, which may or may not mean something. The views along this trail are very special. The vistas in the east end of the Canyon are wide and deep with the river making big turquoise turns along towering, red walls. We look down at the "virgin's leap", a name we gave this sheer drop-off to the river years ago. Unkar Rapids frosts the blue river with white rooster tails.

Up and up over rocks, then easy walking, and then more rocks as we climb towards the Cockscomb, a ridge of skyscraper-type rocks which soar into the blue sky. Looks like a lost city. We skirt below the city and then we are on the high point of the trail. In the east we look back at the Cardenas campsite and to the west is our destination, where the walls are higher and the river more narrow. Going down is a fine walk. We meet the fellow we saw yesterday. He and his very slow buddy are doing the same trip as we, but going out faster. There has been no one else on the trail.

Randy remembers his almost disastrous solo trip years ago. He shows me where he followed a misplaced cairn and went down the wrong drainage. It's dangerously steep and he continued down and came to an impassable drop-off before he realized this wasn't the trail. Panic set in, he was nearly out of water and it was very hot and getting late. He sat down trying to be calm and, being an avid birdwatcher, noticed some birds further down gathered together. He followed them and discovered they had found water. By depressing his spoon in the ground he also found water! It was a long process to fill a canteen, but then he knew he could make it back to look for the correct drainage to Escalante. Just thinking about how close he came to tragedy hit home as I give him a big hug!

On to Escalante. A steep wall to descend and into the dry riverbed. My Sherpa takes my pack and it's a snap. We reach the river and find a nice spot under a huge tamarisk tree. We wash up in the river, rinsing out shirts and socks. We had noticed mare's-tails in the blue sky earlier, which usually means a change. Without a weather report we play it safe and put up the tent, just in case. Sure enough, as we snooze away on our ground cloths, the first drops hit. Randy's tent is a bit cramped for two, but we hurry into it, stumbling in the dark.

FOURTH DAY

Morning arrives with a questionable weather outlook. Randy lights his sage stick and announces it is going to be a great day. We are going to Seventyfive Mile Canyon, an easy jaunt with time for relaxation on its fine, long, sandy beach.

As we climb out of Escalante Canyon it begins to rain. On goes the rain gear as it begins to get more serious. We wait for a while under an overhang as I question Randy's proclamation about it being a great day. Finally we head for the entrance of the deep, dry creekbed of Seventyfive Mile. As we look down into the canyon, it is ominous and dark with walls over 200 feet high on either side. We reach the entrance and my memory is rudely awakened by the sudden drop-off into the canyon where packs must be lowered, footholds must be found, before a jump down to the dry streambed below. But today, the smooth lip of Seventyfive Mile has a stream of water pouring over it. We go down and look it over. It looks wet and slick to me, and working one's way down would be a very damp operation. We decide to wait it out and climb to higher ground under a slight overhanging rock just as the heavens let loose. Rolling thunder bounces back and forth across the canyon walls, lightning bolts crack too close for comfort. The rain increases, mixed with hail. Suddenly we hear the awesome sound of rockfall and we look upcanyon as boulders tumble down from both sides. It's obvious how canyons are formed as we watch Mother Nature let out all the stops. We are dry as we crouch under the overhang, but just a little nervous wondering how many rocks above us are ready to bounce over our heads.

Very suddenly the rain ceases and a weak sun is trying to break through the clouds. Our hopes rise and we decide to wait awhile to see if the water lets up over the drop-off to Seventyfive Mile. Maybe we can get there today after all.

As we look down into the canyon, wondering how soon things will dry out, there is an incredible roar! Upcanyon a wall of red, foaming water has arrived from the uppermost reaches of the long Seventyfive Mile Canyon and is boiling over the drop-off to the canyon below us. A delayed flash flood is sending boulders and rocks and a tremendous amount of water roaring into Seventyfive Mile. We are spellbound as we watch this astonishing wall of red water spilling over into the canyon, filling the narrow streambed with rushing water. We can hear the boulders as they bounce down the smooth rock entrance to the canyon. It continues, never letting up as we watch fascinated and a bit awestruck as we realize we could have been in that canyon when the flash flood arrived.

As we watch this canyon show, the two hikers of yesterday appear. One comes over and tells us that they missed the turnoff and drop into Seventyfive Mile and have been thrashing around on a dead-end trail trying to find a way to the river. Now, dripping wet and frustrated, they have retraced their steps. The flood has diminished some, but the canyon is filled with red water of unknown depth. They are anxious to be on their way. Randy tells them about the alternative route down. We saw a cairn earlier and Randy decides to try it without a pack. It looks terrifying to me. He is out of sight but calls up saying it is doable. He comes out of the hole and persuades me to try it. Unwillingly, I climb down, outcropping rock to outcropping rock, with my eye on some relatively flat land before the final drop to the creekbed. There I find a Canyon favorite, the sacred datura bush with prickly pods full of seeds. The Indians found its

Sacred Datura

blossoms halluci-
nogenic, and years
ago I actually grew
one in my green-
house from seeds I
brought from the
Canyon. I pocket a
seed pod as I climb
back up .

The two hikers
have decided they
will go for it. One
is considering
wearing three pairs
of socks, taking off
his boots to keep them dry. The other fellow is just looking
totally bewildered and probably wondering why he ever
decided to hike the Canyon. As for us, I've made the decision—it's back to Escalante to camp and we'll try again tomorrow. Randy even agrees as we return the two miles back.

The weather is once again deteriorating as we look for
higher ground to pitch the tent. We cover the packs with
plastic bags and Randy rigs up a very artistic shelter with
tamarisk poles and the blue tarp, optimistically planning to
sit under it while a gentle rain falls. Instead we rush into the
tent as the thunder begins its bowling game overhead and
the lightning crackles. Then the rain and wind really begin.
So far we are dry and warm in the confined quarters of
Randy's small tent. I try to read as the wind tears at the nylon rainfly, and the lightning zaps the land too close for comfort. It is only 3:30 P.M. but it seems like 6:00 P.M. I continue
to read as Randy dozes. The light is fading, reading becomes

impossible so I try to nap. Time goes on as it always does. Dinner is out of the question, so we nibble on crackers and granola in our little haven from the elements.

At around 10:00 P.M. we realize the wind has died down and the rain has let up. There is even a faint star trying to break through the dark clouds. Thankfully, we leave the tent, attend to nature's calls, stretch our legs, brush our teeth and head back to our confinement for the rest of the night. Dreams of water and blocked canyons keep me entertained, but at last all is quiet outside and deep sleep takes over.

FIFTH DAY

Morning is a mixture of sunshine and clouds. We pack up the soggy tarp and soaking tent. Everything weighs twice as much. A saucy black raven arrives as breakfast is eaten. She entertains us with a vocabulary of strange calls and sounds, urging us to hurry and be on our way, but hopefully leaving a tidbit or two. When a canyon wren sings its fragile, fall song, I suddenly know that all is well with the world and today will be a great one.

We return once again to the entrance of Seventyfive Mile Canyon, decide on the upper lip of the canyon for our journey down, rather than the steep and tricky rock climb alternative route. The water has stopped except for a small trickle going over the edge. The streambed looks fairly dry with only a few red pools visible. What a change from yesterday! No more roaring red water or boulders bouncing around. All is peaceful as the sky turns a brilliant blue. Everything is fresh and well scrubbed as we tie ropes to our packs and I then lower them to Randy who has dropped to the canyon bottom. I slip over the edge, finding convenient little finger holes to break the drop into the creekbed. We walk through the curving canyon with its towering walls, remembering how it had looked yesterday with its torrent of red water rushing through it. But today the sun slips in now and then and it's very beautiful. The forces of water throughout the centuries cut this deep cleft in the earth, leaving the rocks smooth and carved like fine pieces of art. We come to a deep pool that we can't get around. Off go the packs and my friendly Sherpa provides a boothold, and I'm down into the creekbed again without having to be immerged in that deep, red pool of water.

We reach the long beach of Seventyfive Mile Canyon. It is empty. Too late for recreational rafters, and few hikers do this trail. Very understandable, it's hardly the Bright Angel Trail! Sitting in the sand in a warm sun, we snack and watch the river go by. Ahead is Papago, definitely not my favorite place, but to get to Hance Beach, it must be dealt with. We pick our way over the large rocks above the beach. Randy suggests we look again (this is the third time I've done this trail, the fourth for Randy) at the reason for the Papago detour. It's a gigantic rock which protrudes into the river with the only way around by raft or up and over. Without that handy raft, we face the sheer wall of dark rock with small ledges here and there for handholds. I keep thinking about Brant Calkins' story of his companion who, while climbing up this wall, reached up and was bitten on the hand by a rattlesnake. Hopefully, since it's quite cool here in the shade, the snakes are still comatose and not interested in unsuspecting hands.

Randy goes first and pulls up my pack as I try to steady it while hanging on with fingers and toes to protruding pieces of rock. He is incredibly strong, having to deal with not only his own heavy pack, but mine too while giving advice to his old mom and trying to convince me this is all great fun! I take a quick side-glance down to the river over a hundred feet below—it's a tremendous view, but I can't really

Monarch Butterfly

appreciate it in my present position. The old adrenaline has pumped up and it's always exciting to complete a job that you've been dreading. But it's not quite completed yet. We climb on to the top where the view to the river and Hance Rapids is really spectacular. We must be 200 feet above the river. The problem is we have to get down that 200 feet. In front of us is the fearful boulder and scree scope dipping down at about a forty-five degree angle. It's okay for a while as Randy goes slowly ahead.

Then I reach a bottleneck and I'm forced to remove my pack which keeps getting caught on rocks. My pack is an old rigid one and Randy has a soft climbing one that works on this type of terrain. So once again I call on my wilderness guide who takes my pack and, more or less, drags it down. As I look down this miserable chute, I wonder what in the world possesses this 72-year old female to do this—I should be home knitting! One solution seems to be to sit down in the worst spots. I'm closer to earth, always an environmentalist at heart. Finally, the worst is over and I put my pack back on and finish the climb down. The trail then climbs over rocks and through tamarisks for a mile or so, and we reach a beautiful camping site just above Hance Rapids under a spreading acacia tree with dark, gnarled limbs and tiny, delicate, green, fernlike leaves. We cook up some ramen noodles, the meal we didn't have last night, and relish it in the sun and shade. The worst is behind me. I feel somewhat smug, but mostly just relieved.

A whole lazy afternoon is waiting. Wet bags, tent and clothes are also waiting in our packs from last night's rain. The sun is hot and the acacia tree provides long thorns for hang-

Sand Verbena

ing. Randy has curled up for his afternoon nap. I take my journal and head to the edge of the river, prop up against an ancient river rock and write my memoirs deep in the Grand Canyon, a most desirable place to be. Hance Rapids, with its boat-eating hole, roars in its customary fashion. Monarch butterflies add their delicate beauty to the coyote willow before they migrate to Mexico. Amazing to think that those fragile little wings can get them so far. I walk up the sand dunes along the beach, find a few late sand verbena blossoms, that delightful little plant that hugs the sand and in the spring perfumes the entire beach.

Tonight there's time to cook, so it's gourmet camp food. Noodles with Alfredo sauce, a rehydrated medley of vegetables and Senegalese soup. El Tovar chefs can't top that! No more tent life tonight. It's back to the tarp under the stars. It's quite cool and the old red, down bag feels good. The sky is brilliant with stars. Now and then a plane's lights can be seen high above, the pilot probably saying, "And below is one of the wonders of the world, the Grand Canyon." How lucky to be right in its depths and not on a plane headed for Vegas.

SIXTH DAY

Chilly this morning. All that rain saturated the sand and once again we need to wait for the sun to dry things out. Surprise, the river has turned red. The Little Colorado, eighty miles away, has probably drained into the Colorado along with runoff from all the side canyons, changing its color from clear blue to muddy red. Our water bottles look like cafe au lait as we line them up to let the sediment settle. Meanwhile, hot fruit and oatmeal taste good in a damp camp. The sun is just reaching the shore and I'm headed down to welcome it and get warmed up. The cocoa river churns and froths as it roars through Hance Rapids. A tiny lizard stretches out on a warm rock to join me in soaking up the solar rays.

Today, we leave the river to hike six miles to Hance Creek. It will be our last night, and the first away from the old Colorado River. Steep climbing with views to the river below brings out my new little camera, which Murray gave me, instead of that heavy one I've carried in the past. Randy points out the level the river had reached before it was tamed by Glen Canyon Dam. What a wild river it must have been! Spring meant that impossible high water and summer storms created floods. It was an unpredictable, unruly and frightening river much of the time. Incredible that John Wesley Powell made it through its uncharted water and lived to tell about it. Even now it is awesome in some the rapids. Several rate a #10, the most challenging. Someday, I'd like to do another river trip, just to feel the rhythm of the water and the Canyon.

No more views below. We are in a meadow of gigantic blocks of dark rocks cluttering the land. Something eons ago caused them to tumble down from above. Wonder if an earth tremor caused it? Today and tomorrow we will be coming from the river at 2,000 feet above sea level to over 7,000 feet on the South Rim, which means a lot of up. A perfect day with long vistas from the rosy reds of the high cliffs and pinnacles to the mauves and blue-greys of the deep Inner Gorge. Doesn't look too inviting this time of the year when the sun hardly reaches the dark red river.

We are walking on the pleasant Tonto Platform which is on top of the Tapeats Formation which begins at Hance Rapids and goes all the way past South Bass Canyon to Garnet Canyon where the Tapeats disappears. Easy hiking between the blackbrush which reach out with sharp claws for bare legs. Silver-grey brittlebush dot the landscape. In the spring they are ablaze with brilliant yellow blossoms. We follow wide curves with steep little pitches into the head of small canyons and then back to the big views and cool breezes. A few mare's-tails drift across the blue sky — a small reminder that there could be a change in the weather. We are especially suspect, since before the last storm, mare's-tails were very prominent.

Through Mineral Canyon where the old burro tracks are still very visible. The burros are long gone, which is a great improvement. Vegetation is coming back, which benefits the native wildlife, bighorn sheep in particular. A touch of heat now and then, but this has been a cool and pleasant trip. We make the turn into Hance Canyon, looking down into its rugged depths. Hard to believe that in its upper reaches there are pleasant campsites and a clean stream. Soon as I spot the water below, I pour out the silty red water of the river, looking forward to little Hance Creek for a clear drink. I remember these long stretches thinking the end will never come, and then suddenly a short drop and we are among the familiar acacia trees and setting up camp. The crickets are serenading on our last night, always a nostalgic one. One more night of sleeping on the ground with the sky spread out above with its usual galaxy of stars. Another wonderful trip with many more Canyon memories filed away for further flashbacks.

SEVENTH DAY

A long haul today up to the rim, so we leave early to climb out of Hance Canyon, heading for Redbud Spring, which for some unfortunate reason has been renamed Page Spring. It's a magical spot in spring when the redbud trees are in bloom and the water drops through maidenhair ferns into the small pool below. I gather seeds from the dangling dark red pods and will try my luck at growing a redbud in my little greenhouse. Randy filters water for the trip out. Up the Redwall, an easy Redwall here.

We pass an old mine surrounded with rusted old machinery. It was pick and shovel work in those days, looking for copper or other precious metals. Apparently no great deposits were ever found throughout the Canyon and the rugged miners left or, like Hance and Boucher, turned to escorting tourists while entertaining them with tall tales. There was an old asbestos mine developed by Hance across the river. High upon the steep hillside there is still a trail to the mine site, which we hiked from a river trip. A truly amazing feat for Hance to have hauled asbestos by mule down to the river, where it eventually made its way to Europe to be used for theater curtains.

One more steep burst up the last of the Redwall and on to the more gentle Horseshoe Mesa. Around the old copper mine on the mesa, with its telltale blue and turquoise rocks still mixed in the mine tailings. I find a nice sunny spot under a twisted juniper tree, heavy with silver berries. Breakfast is brunch with a Mexican omelet I've saved for the final day. With stewed fruit, it's pretty fancy fare. We still have seen only those two backpackers since the first day, a week ago. No snakes, probably too cool for them, and only a few lizards scurrying from one warm rock to another.

Three miles to the rim, the last lap, and very, very up. Even though the temperature is cool, sweat pours from my head as I drain my water bottle quickly. Finally civilization begins to intrude as we meet a few day hikers and some who are camping overnight on the mesa. A lunch stop of rehydrated basmati rice, hummus and crackers. A canyon wren, the epitome of the Grand Canyon, sings almost a springlike song, the last call of summer as winter slowly slips into the Canyon. Suddenly I'm freezing cold as my wet shirt and head cools quickly as clouds fill the blue sky. Time to get moving up the steep switchbacks. This trail back in the late 1880s was built by the miners to haul out copper, and then was used as a tourist route for the guests of the Grandview Hotel which was built on the rim after mining folded. The views from every switchback definitely are "grand". The clouds have moved in and the whole Canyon seems subdued and a bit melancholy. Purples, muted pinks and red with deep blue shadows leave the distant mesas and pinnacles in a hushed expectant mood. The rim is getting closer and the air is getting much colder as I near the 7,400-foot elevation of Grandview Point. I round a corner and meet a friendly family with small children who have hiked down a ways. So glad some tourists get to capture the magic of the Canyon by going only a short ways off the tourist scene on the rim.

One last switchback with a good-bye to the Canyon. Far east in the distance can be seen the wide bends of the now red river and the beach at Tanner, our first night's campsite. Seems so far away even as the raven flies, not even considering all the ups and downs and obstacles between here and there. It always seems a little like a dream to think we actually did it. It is truly a Grand Canyon, not to mention all the hundreds of smaller canyons within it, which even by themselves could qualify for scenic attractions or even National Parks. It is definitely a wonder of the world!

We are now on the rim and it's freezing cold. Our car is ten miles away at Lipan Point. I hold up a sign saying "need ride 10 miles east to pick up my car". Randy takes the packs and waits in the trees. Two mangy creatures with large packs is enough to scare off any possible ride. I smile as the tourists walk by giving me strange looks. Here I am looking like a little old lady in need of a helping hand and I'm being ignored! About the time I decide to get more aggressive and drop the little old lady routine, the pleasant family I chatted with below offers me a ride. Nice people from New Jersey, taking their kids to see the West. The Vanagon is waiting safe and sound, and I drive back to pick up Randy and the packs. The wind is blowing and rain is threatening. Our timing is perfect and once again those mare's-tails were a good weather predictor. No camping at Mather Campground tonight. We will live it up at the Maswick Lodge with dinner at El Tovar.

As the service plates are presented by the bowing waiter, and the red wine served in crystal goblets, it's a bit strange to remember the last six nights of eating by candle lantern on a tarp in the sand. This is a treat, but I still think instant mashed potatoes covered with mushroom soup in a Sierra Club cup while listening to the rhythm of the Colorado River is much more special in life's experiences.

Ending

Eight years ago, my last backpack appeared to be my farewell to Grand Canyon trips, but the lure and the memories of this very special place was always with me. Randy, my son, was busy with his life, Murray had joined the spirits of the Canyon and aging friends had no interest in entering this magical hole in the earth with me. But then on my 80th birthday, April 1, 2000, Randy and his friend Suzane invited me for a week's camping trip on the South Rim with the opportunity to day-hike some of our favorite trails. What an exciting birthday present!

We began with the popular Kaibab Trail. The minute I stepped off the rim, there was the familiar thrill of looking down into the Grand Canyon, over the buttes, mesas and pinnacles, all in their proper places with a warm rosy glow illuminating these familiar landmarks. The red dirt dusted my boots, the sun was hot on my old white hat and, just as I had wished, the canyon wren sent its lyrical song cascading through space. It was as though I had never left.

The temperature was hot, the lizards scurried over the rocks looking for shade. Familiar sweat poured down my face, blurring my dark glasses, as we searched out fat juniper and pinion trees to rest under during the trek. At every stop I looked intently at the Canyon views trying to etch themselves in my mind for future memories. It was a wonderful trip down memory lane and an 80th birthday gift to remember forever. But then there is always next year!

My thanks to all of you who have vicariously walked these trails with me throughout this book. And, for those who have already backpacked in the Grand Canyon, perhaps you have enjoyed reliving your experiences. For those of you who plan someday to do the same, I hope I've managed to convey part of the wonderment which awaits you.

The Canyon is now part of my life. The experiences of over 250 days I've spent within it will continue to reward me with memories I shall never forget. To go into the Canyon, trip after trip, east end to west end, north side and south side and to know it so well is something I will always cherish. I've seen the Canyon in all its moods, I've agonized under blazing sun as the miles stretched endlessly on. I've been drenched and battered by storms, snow has flattened my tent in November, I've bounced through the rapids in a rubber raft, and my boots have waded through deep snow climbing to the rim. I've been bruised and scratched, thirsty and exhausted, and I've been overcome with the beauty, the austerity, the mystery, and the silence.

The miles of walking, in and out of side canyons, each with its own ecosystem and personality, the vistas filled with strangely shaped pinnacles and towers with names like Zoroaster, Vishnu Temple, Wotan's Throne, Angel's Gate, and mesas and canyons where no one has ever set foot, are all part of the magic. I've seen sunsets from incredible places and watched the Canyon turned fiery red, and the purples of the depths below awakened to a desert sunrise. I've seen moonlight bathe the cliffs in silver and watched the sunlight splash on wet pinnacles after a rainstorm. It's all there, filed away in my memory. And on long, winter evenings this magic returns and fills me with peace and contentment.

Finally, when my feet will no longer carry me into and out of the Canyon, I will probably still return and find a nice, flat, warm rock, just below the rim, where I'll sit and watch the changing moods of this special place. And when I leave this mortal world, who knows? My spirit may soar with the ravens as we swoop over the chasms below and finally perch on Angel's Gate for a bird's eye view of the Canyon. Then, as we fly down again and over the heads of some weary hikers, I'll give an unearthly chuckle as I soar across those never-ending sinuosities, propelled only by the wind!

As I sit in my little, solar house, high on a sunny hillside in Old Snowmass, Colorado, it's a satisfying feeling to know that this book has been written. Selfish, of course, for me, but more important, I hope it will be a message to all who read it, that the Grand Canyon is a special place and, although we may think that it is protected by being a National Park, there are always threats. More dams can be built, mining can, and already does, create air and water pollution, bridges over the river can be constructed, more planes will be flying over-head, and additional commercialization can spoil the Canyon's integrity.

So as my potbelly stove crackles merrily, and I write this final chapter in the snowy, Colorado mountains, my plea goes out to everyone who cares about the Grand Canyon, to be alert to these threats and to do everything possible to pro-tect this wonder of the world so that, as the years go by, we can all be assured that the sun will rise and set over a Grand Canyon that only nature will control, preserving its eternal silent grandeur for generations to love and appreciate.